IN PRAISE
of
houseflies

MEDITATIONS ON THE GIFTS IN
EVERYDAY QUANDARIES

ELISE TEGEGNE

CALLA PRESS
PUBLISHING

In Praise of Houseflies: Meditations on the Gifts in Everyday Quandaries

Copyright © 2025 by Elise Tegegne

Published by Calla Press Publishing
Texas Countryside
United States 76401

Cover Design: Samantha Cabrera
First Printing, 2025
Printed in the USA

Unless otherwise indicated, Scripture quotations are from the ESV Bible (The Holy Bible, English Standard Version), copyright © 2001 by Crossway, a publishing ministry of Good News Publishers.

All emphases in Scripture quotations have been added by the author.

Trade paperback ISBN: 978-1-966828-03-7

Wisdom arrives over time, and nearly always as a result of quiet choices made in the midst of affliction. In her essay collection, *In Praise of Houseflies*, Elise Tegegne offers hard-won insight into how even our sufferings—exile, isolation, privation, humiliation, loss, pain, and grief—might be recognized as the very means by which the soul becomes a *trusting* and *trustworthy* source of stillness and of peace.

—**Scott Cairns**, author of *The End of Suffering: Finding Purpose in Pain*

This book is a blessing—an elegant reminder of how grace is threaded through the day, always available—especially in challenges, annoyances and disappointments. Elise's lively reflections range from small moments of insight to rich stories of how God shows up "lovely in limbs, lovely in eyes not his." Her openness to receiving that grace and sharing it, and the ways she calls in the wisdom of spiritual writers and teachers are timely encouragements to live into hard moments with hope and confident prayer and expectation of adventure.

—**Marilyn McEntyre**, author of *Caring for Words in a Culture of Lies*

Tegegne's tender book is soaked in grace. Through this poetic and vulnerable work, she finds the ordinary grace, not simply in everyday moments, but in that which annoys us and makes us uncomfortable; humiliation, loneliness and pain. Tegegne embraces the undesirable, as an opportunity, to shape her soul and grow in her love and understanding for our God. You will find yourself asking, as her mother does, "Isn't this gracious of God?"

—**Shemaiah Gonzalez**, author of *Undaunted Joy: The Revolutionary Act of Cultivating Delight*

My favorite writing blends insightful observations and commentary along with lovely turns of phrase. Elise Tegegne reflects deeply on life as an expat abroad for a time, being a young mother, reflecting as spiritual pilgrim on humiliation and loneliness, and meeting God in the ordinary, routine, and even annoying—always with lyrical phrasing. She composes masterfully memorable aphorisms and her attention to lists, daily details, and real life are rendered in poetic prose. She is one of my favorite writers.

—**Arthur Boers**, Anglican priest in Toronto and author of *Shattered: A Son Picks Up the Pieces of His Father's Rage* (Eerdmans, 2023)

With luminous prose, Elise Tegegne reveals the quiet power woven through the fullness of our days. *In Praise of Houseflies* gently invites readers to embrace disruptions and difficulties as a sacred practice, discovering meaning and transformation in the rhythms of daily life, even when events unfold contrary to our hopes. Tegegne uncovers hidden holiness in the unexpected, showing how every moment can brim with grace and possibility.

—**Charlotte Donlon**, author of *The Great Belonging: How Loneliness Leads Us to Each Other*

With tender prose and piercing beauty, *In Praise of Houseflies* invites us to catch the divine in the moments we least expect to. This whispered collection of meditations is a quiet sieve, a call to reimagine our daily inconveniences as holy ground. If you've ever wondered how to seek God in the endless drudgery, may Elise's words sift into your soul—and stay.

—**Erin Loechner**, author of *Chasing Slow*

It takes a writer of extraordinary attentiveness to incarnate the transcendence of the ordinary. This book of essays by Elise Tegegne is a gift of wonder and a hymn of praise. I'll never go to the dentist's waiting room without it.

—**Father Michael Rennier**, author of *The Forgotten Language: How Recovering the Poetics of the Mass Will Change Our Lives* and editor at *Dappled Things*

For Yene fikroch

contents

Ineluctable necessity, misery, distress, the crushing weight of poverty and of work that drains the spirit, cruelty, torture, violent death, constraint, terror, sickness—all these are God's love!

—Simone Weil, Gravity and Grace

It is a paradox of human life that in worship, as in human love, it is in the routine and the everyday that we find the possibilities for the greatest transformation.

—Kathleen Norris, The Quotidian Mysteries

introduction

We must not wish for the disappearance of any of our troubles, but grace to transform them.

—Simone Weil, Gravity and Grace

In February 2020, I sat buckled on a flight to a writer's retreat, little knowing I was enjoying my last few moments of pre-pandemic freedom. Inside the sky-bound cabin, an epiphany struck: *What would it look like if we flipped everyday annoyances on their heads? What if, instead of avoiding them, we embraced them, seeking the gifts they hid?* I wondered what it might be like to try the "method of investigation" French philosopher Simone Weil once noted: "As soon as we have thought something, try to see in what way the contrary is true."[1]

Unprepared for epiphanic grace, I pulled out my phone (the only device at hand) and brainstormed things most humans avoid: from elevator music and bee stings and lipstick on teeth, to funerals and house fires and robbery. I entitled the list "In Praise Of," wondering what treasures I could find if I viewed what most of us call "problems" as gifts to be praised. How little I knew that just a month later, the whole world would turn apocalyptic; millions would die; the challenges of everyday quandaries would be exponentially magnified.

Over the next three years, I wrote essays on the most pressing topics from my brainstormed list. They loosely follow a few key seasons in my life: four years teaching French at an international mission school in Addis Ababa, Ethiopia; the pandemic lockdown; the early years of marriage; and motherhood. Though I have arranged the essays in roughly chronological order, they do not necessarily represent a linear progression of thought and can be enjoyed in any order.

Though I began planning the book around the pandemic's outbreak, the seeds of its conception were planted long before I consciously realized it. Looking back, I see the principal sowers as my parents. Just the other day, my dad told me that recounting noticings of divine grace in the grit of daily life is "one of your mom and my favorite things to do."

My mom has a way of finding the unique beauty in things most people find distasteful. As an elementary school student, she ended up seeing the heart behind a gruff teacher most students disliked. She loves rainy days, and adulthood hasn't dimmed her delight in snow. When delays or missed turns or kinks unfold in everyday plans, her eyes alight with the anticipation of adventure. But most of all, she loves spotting God's abundant, uncanny care in the weave of everyday life. During my earliest years of childhood, my family was poor enough to have qualified for food stamps (though I never knew a moment without plenty). When my dad got a significant raise at a new job, she said she was almost sad; she would miss God's miraculous provision in living a life consciously close to the brink of need.

My father's continual song is God's nearness, God's besotted closeness to us in everyday life. A poet and philosopher, he is always attuned to what challenges teach. When I ask him how he is doing in the midst of his too-often migraines or the occasional illness, his response is, by typical human standards, unusual. Rather than express complaint or anger or resistance, he says in his humble, quiet way how he is listening for what God is telling him in the pain. This consistent modeling has profoundly shaped how I view life's everyday quandaries.

The essays in this book are not comprehensive studies. They are, in the tradition of writers like Montaigne and Charles Lamb, meditations that meander, flit, and pause. Furthermore, my experiences are limited to my frame of reference as a middle-class, white American perched in a wealthy corner of the West. My conception of "everyday quandary" might be vastly different from that of someone just diagnosed with cancer or a refugee living in my husband's home country of Ethiopia. Compared to displacement, war, famine, deadly disease, and other upheavals, my experiences of challenges are rather narrow in scope.

Thus from the book's inception, I decided to write from what I know and remain largely within the bounds of the everyday, rather than uncover the grace in life-altering trauma as do many other excellent books (though I do hazard ginger steps into darker themes). In the tradition of writers like Emily Dickinson, who famously lived as a recluse, I have sought to eke out some universal truths from the banalities of quotidian existence. To find the glory shimmering in the nooks and crannies of unwashed dishes and heaps of laundry and the relentless rhythm of routine.

In focusing on everyday challenges, this book does not venture directly into the realm of theodicy. (I leave that to the theologians.) In addition, the book does not seek to romanticize, underestimate, or belittle pain's devastating effects. Pain is brutal and roots in the fundamental brokenness of the world. Rather than paint over pain with sunny hues, I've tried to look it full in the face. And in looking (closely, carefully), I've found glimmers of grace there. And it is this grace that I have sought to unearth. Somehow, in a mystery beyond my wildest fathoming, God redeems the irreparable, and I am learning to have eyes for this unexpected redemption. Each of the essays in this book is an attempt at practicing this redeemed vision, an exercise in refining a lens for viewing the daily quandaries of queues and questions, loneliness and longing.

And it is an invitation for readers to do the same. So, dear reader: I welcome you to pause, take a deep breath, and attune your spirit to God as you open these pages. My prayer is that God would guide you to a refreshed perspective on the dailiness of life, that you might see the glimmerings of divine tracery wherever you look: in the dentist's waiting room, the early morning alarm, the gridlock traffic, the housefly. That you might, as the Preacher says, *make [your] soul see good.*[2]

Oh, there is so much good to see.

Elise Tegegne
Indianapolis, 2024

Part One:
Pilgrimage

body laid bare:

on
humiliation

Humility (n.), humiliation (n.): From Latin humilis *"lowly, humble," literally "on the ground," from* humus *"earth."*

When we recognize that we can no longer rely on our own resources, we open a space for God to work.

—*Desmond Tutu and Mpho Tutu,* Made for Goodness

Perhaps the scene goes like this. Mountain light refracts off the fifteen or so desks arranged horseshoe-style before the whiteboard. Tea time is over at the international mission school in Addis Ababa, Ethiopia, and the children have all unhooked themselves from the jungle gym outside the window. Now my three eleventh-grade French students stare at me with an expression I do not try to understand. I can feel the lemon bar I ate begin to sag in my stomach, while the Nescafé unnerves me to a jittery edge. Or maybe I'm simply nervous.

"*Voici le pronom relatif le plus difficile*," I say, writing *dont*, one of the most difficult French relative pronouns, on the board. Even I find it difficult, but I do not say this. I do not mention that I spent my tea time alone in the classroom, re-reading my notes between quick, sticky bites. I do not mention that I'm new to all this. They can tell.

Just months ago, I graduated from university with a double major in English and French. My dream was to teach English in a French-speaking country, but I ended up teaching French in a largely English-speaking one. (Although Amharic is Ethiopia's official language, public-school instruction is given in English from secondary school onwards.) According to the mission organization that sent me, I am a missionary, but mostly I feel I am a failure.

Teaching here has been like drowning every day, every day thrashing to keep my nostrils above the waves. It's the longest I've ever been away from my family and my first time teaching and my first time on the continent of Africa and my first time in a high school French classroom. As a home-schooler, my only formal French education was at university. I am making this up as I go.

Perhaps I'm wearing my red skirt, the hand-me-down one with the broken zipper that doesn't stay up. Against the pressure of my belly, the rise and fall of breath, the zipper slowly inches open and more open, until I finally realize it's three inches cracked open. I suck in and re-zip.

In the classroom, I write example sentences with *dont* on the board. My three students are attentive and respectful, as usual. The mission community calls them MKs: missionary kids. Two of them speak Amharic with relative fluency, and the other speaks Mursi, the language of a people in Southern Ethiopia. They have seen faces like mine before: bright and smiley world-changers who cycle in and out of the school every few years (or less). The school is chronically understaffed, always recruiting.

Their intelligence, and perhaps experience in this country, intimidate me. They ask questions I oftentimes cannot answer, especially the slender Finn with the angular glasses, the one a wrinkly science teacher deemed with all seriousness, "Not a genius, but very bright."

I continue explaining in French, trying to recall this lecture from my recent university days. "*Dont* can mean 'whose' or 'about which' or 'about whom.'"

The Finnish kid raises his hand. There is a certain gleam in his eyes that belies his respectful demeanor. I would have taken a deep breath, but my slipping zipper restricts me. Here we go. "How would you say, 'The child whose football about which we speak is thrown?'"

I stare at him for a few seconds, glance at the others. Little glimmers of light reflect off their eyes like giggles. Inside I panic, blank. But I cannot show that. I have not yet learned the wisdom of telling students, "I don't know," and then finding the answer together. I have also not yet learned that when a student asks a question, especially one you are not sure of, a useful tactic is to ask a question in return in order to allow students to think through solutions on their own (or just to buy you time). Breathing in, I project my most confident of faces, whip around to the board and write out the sentence. Even as I write, I know something is wrong. I know I am teaching them lies.

"*Voilà!*" I turn back, wondering if they will buy it: the answer I've written and the confidence with which I've written it.

This time the boy with the head of tight blonde coils joins the game. His father is the director of my mission organization in Ethiopia. "But how would you say, 'The child about whom I was thinking whose football is thrown about whom we speak?'" I cannot tell if the one girl in the class has tears in her eyes from frustration or glee.

Fool, I take the challenge again. They are just playing with me now. Around we go in circles. I translate their sentences with all the mock-bravado I can muster, and the students (seeing through the façade?) ask for more. Turning from my students to the whiteboard and back again drives me dizzy.

Perhaps I giggle, a high-pitched, uneasy squeal, in a kind of subconscious attempt to diffuse my terror at being made a fool.

When the bell rings, it is a mercy.

*

I was not used to failing with such gusto.

The spring before the humiliating episode with French relative pronouns, I had swished and swayed with all my ribbons and medals: graduating summa cum laude, with honors, a Presidential Scholar. Like paparazzi, my mom and grandparents had snapped photos of my glamorous smile. At my graduation party, my awards (some taken down from the wall behind my bedroom door, some in gold-filigree folders) filled the dining room table. My high school-aged sister and her friends laughed at how wonderfully ridiculous it was that I had been given so many. I laughed with them as humbly as I could.

In fact, most of my life I had been like Mary Poppins, "practically perfect in every way," as my mother would say with a dash of pride and not a little humor. Other titles I had gathered included "the smartest kid in the class" and "the human dictionary." At the end-of-year awards ceremonies in elementary school, I would amass stacks of certificates in anything from academics to art to athletics. I was proud that I could be good, not just at one thing, but at everything, as it seemed to me. But after returning home from the classroom parties, after the sugar-dive hit and the adrenaline kicked off, I would feel suddenly sad.

My mom was most proud of the little plastic trophy I received at the end of my fifth-grade year: an award for humility. I never bragged, knew gloating was a sin. When the teacher would hand me my test back, with the 101% (because I got the bonus question right, too) and a sticker, I'd inwardly smile and outwardly turn the paper over so no one could see. Perhaps as much as any academic award, I wanted the one for good Christian girls, too.

*

Which I thought I would get becoming a missionary. I thought all my mission training and cultural sensitivity and special calling would elevate me to a kind of ethereal rank. Recalling the "Heroes of the Faith" biographies my mother would read to us kids at bedtime, I thought missionaries were the ultimate in holiness, that they somehow achieved Super Christian status.

Then I became one.

Here I am living on what the missionary community calls "the mission field," grounded in the very same continent David Livingstone evangelized—and my students laugh at me. Like the time I self-consciously tried to show off my Amharic skills by forcing a poorly-pronounced word into a conversation (inciting the derisive chuckles of some ninth-grade girls). Or the time I was trying to vaunt my ability to write in Amharic by inscribing the word for "coffee house" on the board. I later learned the words for "coffee house" was a euphemism for "brothel," and the glee on some of my students' faces, which I mistook for admiration, was probably more like ridicule.

It's my first time failing, and what is worse, failing at something that really matters. I've prayed and fasted and wept and sensed a divine leading to this place. Single-income, coupon-clipping families have pledged monthly donations so that I can be here. I have students who must pass their exams to attend university. The heft of their futures press against my spine, and I am failing them. Or perhaps I feel I am failing myself, not achieving my standard of being exceptional.

My inner perfectionist, that cruel taskmaster, that demon, berates me in the quiet hours after the night has swallowed the sun. *How could you be so stupid? You are such an idiot. You are a failure. You are worthless. You are nothing.*

What brings relief are other people's reactions when I tell them I teach French. They remember nothing from their old French classes, except a song or a phrase. Their teachers have dissolved in their memories. I am banking on the mercy of forgetfulness.

*

Perhaps the most chilling nightmares are not the lucid dreams of drowning in fathomless oceans or of petrifying while monsters breathe at the back of your skull. Perhaps the most chilling nightmares are those that play on our fear of humiliation. Like dreams of public nudity, which have periodically plagued me since childhood. I distinctly recall a dream of being naked at my elementary school, trying to hide behind a small piece of cardboard in the too-bright halls. In those dreams, the thing with which you have to cover yourself is never enough, the clothes you're craving too far away. There is the perilous feeling of revealing what you didn't mean to, what you hoped no one would ever see.

But such dreams are vapor compared with real-life humiliation. It's like the makeup you've caked on your face dissolves in a bucket-splash of cold water. Like being caught without your carefully filigreed fortress, the one you've built with militaristic precision to protect yourself and your most beloved, or most reviled, secrets. Like the broken zipper suddenly opening all the way, body bare-fleshed.

Humiliation has a way of turning your bowels inside out, even as you gag with the reality of being espied. One of the true but shameful parts of you is naked in the day. You're ashamed, not (oftentimes) because of your weakness, but because you got caught in it.

Now somebody knows the secret: *you're not perfect.*

Turns out you're not as smart or as brave or as beautiful as you want everyone to think you are, as you think you are. The moment your friend tells you you've had kale in between your incisors for the past hour, all of the fervor with which you made your arguments over lunch, all your points made, you yourself, all melt into a humbled puddle.

Therein lies humiliation's gift.

*

Mornings in Addis (that city of eye-searing sun) are like this: I am flat down, nose in the carpet. I've had the naked dream, but this time the dream was real. I've revealed my own foolishness. Me, Miss Mary-Poppins-Perfect, in front of an audience without the self-protective layer of knowledge or respect or achievement. De-fortressed, de-masked, de-clothed. I pray for the grace of God with a fervor I've never expressed before.

*

Praying for specific virtues can be one of the riskiest prayers to pray. One day my venerable uncle, who was hosting my family for a beachside vacation, warned, "You'd better be careful when you pray for patience." That evening I dared that prayer and in the morning couldn't walk. Slow, slow, I had to crawl to the bathroom to swallow some ibuprofen. I could barely move most of the day, until my aunt offered her masseuse, who worked a lovely miracle. The connection may have been pure chance. I'd been having lower-back pain for years and sleeping on a stiff bed that night. But it is worth inviting the possibility that the prayer and the pain were linked. That God answers. And that God's answers can terrify.

Though I know the reality of this terror, I am learning to trust God. If the answer hurts (the stiffened back, the nose crushed in the carpet), it hurts because the hurt is good: a bright burning of the dead and the dross. That from the crushed stubble of my prided fortress, I might rise more whole and real.

In my preparation for Ethiopia, I don't think I ever consciously prayed for humility. I knew I struggled with pride. But I don't think I linked this sin with the looming challenge of cross-cultural ministry. I knew I felt inadequate, but I did not know the abysmal depths of my inadequacy. I never fathomed God's capacity for humbling me.

Even though I did not pray the prayer, perhaps Christ, who knew what was best, who knew what I needed, was praying it for me.

*

Though God's image refracts through my frame in a once-in-a-universe way, though I am fearfully and wonderfully made, a wonderful work of God as the poet says, life under the Ethiopian sun has forced me to face the reality of my own mediocrity. I am not as strong or intelligent as I thought. I finger my plans in water. I pray more than I ever have before. At the teacher's meetings while the afternoon sun spears the floating dust, I crouch with pen poised, and while the seasoned teachers talk, I listen.

Simone Weil: "When we force ourselves to fix the gaze, not only of our eyes but of our souls, upon [an] exercise in which we have failed through sheer stupidity, a sense of our mediocrity is borne in upon us with irresistible evidence. No knowledge is more to be desired."[1]

A gift: the broken red skirt and the nonsense-scribbled whiteboard and the adolescent giggles. Knowledge to be desired above all else: the reality of my mediocrity. The reality of your own—give it your bravest gaze.

Why is it so hard to accept my own mediocrity? Why must I insist on being glorified, a goddess in a universe of my own making?

Even the God who made the universe gave up all his throne-room glory.

*

This is what I know of humbling: my mother sits down next to me, her tears gleaming in the evening lamplight. She tells me how church friends, soft-spoken, kind-eyed folk I barely know, just committed to give monthly towards my salary in Addis Ababa. Prior to making this commitment, the husband had lost his job.

Everyone who gave, gave with a sense of sacrifice. None are what most Americans would call rich.

Such extravagant grace—bread from heaven fallen like deep snow over the ground—presses me deep in the gut. Reverberations echo through my body like a gentle quake: *I—the proud one, the mediocre one—do not deserve this.*

But on my tongue is the taste of honey.

*

This is what I know of humiliation: the stall door sways open in my elementary school bathrooms and a pony-tailed girl in my class peeks through, smirking at my half-naked body stooped on that porcelain bowl. She does not preserve my dignity by shutting the door or averting her eyes. I cannot reach the door I am helpless I am so so embarrassed. The zipper is undone undone undone.

At this point my memory blacks out.

*

Writing myself into circles of French pronouns or flaunting mispronounced words to adolescent chuckles felt in the moment like humiliation: public events highlighting my foolishness. They kicked me off the illusory pedestal of my own making. Crushed my fortress. Dissolved my mask. Left me bare. Questioned my worth.

Or was it I who questioned my own worth? I suspect the humiliation was much (all?) of my own making. I was the one who believed the lie that failure made me worthless. I was the one who coddled untruths under my covers in the dark. My own perfectionism attacked my divinely-graced belovedness.

Maybe God intended the lesson to humble, but my own pride humiliated.

*

My mentor teacher Alyssa sits alongside me on the benches by the souk built into the school's basement. Our tiny auburn cups of frothy macchiatos glint in the sunlight. I confess my mediocrity, my inability to manage roomfuls of teenagers, let alone impart knowledge to them.

Her voice is gentle, and later on we will gather weekly to pray, that is, to get low, on the ground, to grace-gather. Perhaps she was the first one who told me, "Give yourself grace." Whatever her words, I feel peace blooming inside.

To receive divine grace, my hands must be open like hungry blooms bent skyward. My knees must be grounded. And how sweet the balm to my perfectionism-chapped soul, when at last I can receive God's grace, give grace to myself.

*

Perhaps the alchemy of transforming humiliating moments into humbling ones begins with my posture. Embracing my rootedness in the earth (that rich humus, that God-breathed stuff of humanhood, that place of sudden manna) can turn what could be humiliating into what is humbling. I recall the flower of the Sisters of the Holy Family, a Catholic order of African-American nuns living in New Orleans:

> The violet is the emblem of the Congregation. It does not lift its head in haughtiness; its leaves extend upon the ground; it seems to lend itself to being trod upon and has no thorns to protect itself against aggression.
>
> It needs no glass enclosure to protect it from the cold for it endures the cruelest frost and most terrible heat. It grows in all climates; it is difficult for the wind to tear it up, and hurricanes do not break it because it is so lowly.[2]

If I were a violet, I could welcome humbling, even moments that could be humiliating. In some sense, I could, just maybe, be humiliation-proof.

Humbled, yes.

Humble, yes.

But not humiliated.

Here on the ground is where grace gathers, honeyed manna aplenty.

Perhaps if I knew I was low, no one could make me lower. If I was deeply acquainted with my weaknesses and humble and vulnerable about them, it would not be surprising or shameful to be seen in an unflattering light. And if I knew who I was, if I were rooted in my God-named belovedness, then no one could call me unloved. If I were grounded in love, no kale-in-the-teeth or broken zippers or abstruse French pronouns could make me feel unworthy.

Even when crushed under heels, the violets ascend again towards the light.

secret ladder sanctum:

on loneliness

It is this simple matter of seeing loneliness as a gift—to be received, and to be offered back to God.

—Elizabeth Elliot, The Path of Loneliness

Fill up the emptiness of your heart with love for God and your neighbor.

—Edith Stein

My mother sits on the hardwood floor, and I crumple my small body into her lap, crying. It is the end of another school day and I have wandered the pavement alone again at recess and no one wants to be my friend.

*

My otherness oppresses. My intense shyness, my straight A's, my disdain for the preoccupations of elementary school girls—Lip Smackers lip gloss and giggling for no reason and boys—separate me. I am intensely aware of how I am unlike those society has categorized me as like. I recall the Sesame Street song my mother sings in the face of anomaly, "One of these is not like the others; one of these things just doesn't belong."[1]

*

I shelter under paper pages. Books breathe when I open them, spines stretched, the spaces between pages full of air like lungs. Like the best of friends, books speak what is true and make me laugh and sometimes cry (a good kind of cry, like when Old Dan and Little Ann die). It is I who close the covers of a book; they cannot close themselves to me.

*

As a teenager, I no longer cower behind my otherness: I flaunt it. Sitting alone in the back row of the trailer where the junior high youth group meets, I scoff at the rich girls' flat-ironed hair and smooth-shaved legs and wide-open mouths. I am unlike, I say to myself, exulting in my raw curls and second-hand bell-bottoms. These words hold my secret consolation, hide the agony of rejection. I take pride in all the ways I am different, each way another layer plastered between them and me, between my pain and me.

*

Another junior high Sunday sitting in a metal folding chair, alone. Today there is one other girl in the back row. She is blond and, to my distaste, wearing lip gloss. But her face is gentle and she seems to be wearing what I am: hand-me-downs. She sits next to me, says her name and calls forth my own. She offers me her presence and accepts mine. She will be my saving grace for junior high, high school, university. She will remain my friend when I am in Ethiopia and when I return. To me, she is Jesus in skin.

*

I am called to be such a "little Christ" here in this world (writes C.S. Lewis),[2] the only eyes, mouth, hands, feet, and heart Christ has in this world (adds St. Theresa of Avila).[3] If I embodied this truth, I would be much more concerned with consoling than being consoled, understanding than being understood, loving than being loved (prays St. Francis of Assisi).[4] I wonder how my loneliest moments wandering the pavement in grade school or exiling myself in the back row of folding chairs in junior high could have been different had I sought the fringe-dwellers (even the ones hidden in popular garb), rather than sitting alone, pitying myself.

＊

After a high school mission trip to Katrina-wrecked DeLisle, Mississippi, our youth pastor tells us to journal about the experience in our hotel rooms, our last stop before heading home. We have soaked through t-shirts in 100-plus-degree humidity together, gutted weathered homes together, tattooed ourselves with permanent marker together, eaten jambalaya together, prayed by firelight together. As I kneel on the floor in the fusty room next to my opened journal, it hits me for the first time—gut-punchy and soul-releasing like truth does: I need people.

＊

In *No Man Is an Island*, Trappist monk Thomas Merton agrees: my salvation, the "full discovery" of who I really am, the fulfillment of my "own God-given powers"—I cannot find by myself in myself alone. I must find myself through others. Paraphrasing St. Paul, he writes, "Every Christian is part of my own body."⁵

＊

For my masters degree, I am writing an essay that contrasts my frizzy-haired wallflower self with the most beautiful and popular lip-gloss girl of my elementary school class: Brooke. Blonde and slim-limbed, Brooke embodied the beauty of her mother, a professional cheerleader. My mentor comments, "There's always a Brooke! Though the Brookes hate themselves, too."

Her words jangle and jumble inside.

＊

My sister, who did a research study in the Middle East to hear the stories of the misunderstood,[6] found a watchword in this quotation from Elie Weisel, who told the story of his own society's attempts to exterminate him: "We must see in every person a universe with its own secrets, with its own treasures, with its own sources of anguish, and with some measure of triumph."[7]

Every person, not just me.

Every person: the lip-gloss girls and the flat-ironed girls.

Everyone is other.

*

What secrets did Brooke hold, even as I held my own? What were her treasures and triumphs, divine tracings I neglected or refused to see? What were her sources of anguish? How did I need her? How did she need me? Did she feel, beneath her charismatic blue eyes, a loneliness like mine?

*

At my missionary training the summer between graduating from university and leaving the US to teach French in Ethiopia, I hear words I do not forget: "Missionaries are a grieving people." Missionaries gouge out their roots from one land and attempt to transplant them in another. Then they do it again.

I shovel deep, grit staining skin, yank the tracery woven into the patch of earth I called home.

Yank again.

*

Ethiopia is home and not home. America is home and not home. Where do I belong? At a suburban café in my hometown that does not feel mine anymore, I tell another recently-returned missionary, "I've never longed for heaven more than now."

*

"Isn't this the way it is supposed to be?" Søren Kierkegaard might ask from his solitary desk in Copenhagen. He writes, "They call themselves believers and thereby signify that they are pilgrims, strangers, and aliens in the world . . . Faith expressly signifies the deep, strong, blessed restlessness that drives the believer so that he cannot settle down at rest in this world."[8]

Though our bodies entwine in intimate necessity, my mother and Brooke and my friend like my lungs and toes and bones, each of us remains essentially, blessedly alien.

Loneliness, it seems, is part of the believer's calling.

*

It is September 11th, the Ethiopian New Year, and I am walking cobblestone streets in Addis Ababa with my Ethiopian boyfriend to meet his parents for the first time. Amidst this city of chaos, their gardened compound has a preternatural hush, like a secret-ladder sanctum. When I enter the cool home shadowed in feathery leaves, his father says in English, "Welcome home," and his mother, fragrant with Chanel and that deeper fragrance that moves from life to life, wraps me in her arms as if I were born from her own womb.[9]

*

This is what I told myself as a single woman searching for a husband: Plato was wrong when he said that in the beginning humans were two selves in one; that the two selves were once separated; and that we spend our lives looking for our completing other half.[10] I am whole already in God, I said, long-haired, long-skirted missionary that I was. I don't need a man to complete me, I said.

But after feeling the gentle bones of my boyfriend's fingers enlacing mine before the light of an unfolding film, after those star-lit jazz concerts in the nighttime garden, I found this hard to believe. Surely, this man will complete me in a way I've never known before. Surely, he will see the universe in me. And I will no longer feel so alien.

*

The sudden oneness of marriage shocks, and I feel the reverberations daily: sleepless nights learning to share a bed with another body, the jolting pain and pleasure of sex. After the wedding and honeymoon by the sea, my husband does not recognize me. Depressed, sleep-deprived, bone-thin. Befuddled in the fog of new marriage, neither of us understands my change. Enmired in the depths of some strange despair, I cannot rise. I scream and shout and hit myself. I weep against the tiles of the bathroom floor and feel more alone—married—than ever in all my life.

*

When my husband and I join our bodies together, breast to breast, thigh to thigh, I am struck with how feeble our attempts at oneness are. How, at its most intimate, our union is brief: a beautiful breath. How our bones and blood get in the way of becoming truly one.

*

The only advice I remember from our premarital counseling was to give each other space. My husband and I both need time alone: he to watch his movies and I to read my books. I am reminded of philosopher Martin Buber's "I–Thou" relationship, which names the space between us as sacred.

*

Sacred: how my husband's skin is caramel and mine is cream. How he speaks syllables to his Ethiopian family I do not understand; how I speak syllables to my French students he does not understand. How his culture taught him the beauty of interdependence and mine the beauty of independence. How he hears God in the ocean and I hear God in the mountains. How, if the tones of our voices were not different, there would be no chance for harmony.

*

No one will ever understand, fully. No one will ever grasp the secrets, the treasures, the triumph. Not even the anguish, the unique imprint of sorrow that shapes each human heart. No wonder the first verse of Lamentations—a whole book of Scripture dedicated to expressing woe—begins with an image of loneliness: *How lonely sits the city that was full of people!*

*

How lonely, the pilgrim believers of old. Those saints, those set-apart ones.[11] Before building the ark, Noah was *the only blameless person living on earth at the time.*[12] Abraham left his country, his people, and his father's household to go to a land he did not know.[13] Ruth clung to a bitter widow rather than return home, gathered fallen barley heads in a strange land.[14] Plagued with fateful dreams, sold into slavery by his jealous brothers, Joseph lived the rest of his life as an exile in Egypt.[15] Moses grew up an outsider in Pharaoh's palace, walked forty years in wilderness leading a people who often hated him, and ended his days outside the land of milk and honey.[16] Orphaned Esther gave up the only home she knew to be bedded by a pagan king.[17] Israelite officials forced Jeremiah into a muddy cistern for speaking words they found offensive.[18] John the Baptist, that wild man in camel hair, kept house in the desert and was not afraid to call the religious leaders a bunch of snakes.[19]

*

How lonely, Jesus. Of divine nature in a human world. Not good-looking or desirable. Constantly misunderstood (the well-meaning disciples—the few into whom he carefully poured his wisdom, presence, love—nodding and completely missing the point yet again). Nearly pushed off a cliff by neighbors from his own hometown. And at a moment of profound anguish—blood moistening his brow in the midnight garden—his disciples snooze. Then the icy kiss, the crowing cock. Forsaken: by family, friends, community, government, religion, and, in the last moments of breath on the cross, God.

*

A childhood memory: My room is dark, lit only by the hallway light. As she does every night, my mother sits at the edge of my bed and prays with me. She prays I will find a friend. I know she is holding my sorrow as she holds my hand. In my loneliness, she unites me to the High Priest who—knowing ultimate rejection—sympathizes, who understands as even she cannot. She teaches me to pray, to commune with the divine this way, even when she is no longer there.

*

In the midnight dark, I slip up the secret ladder. My Beloved awaits. The One who has searched me and known me from the womb, who knows my every motion and meander, who knows what I will say before I say it, who knows me more than anyone ever could.

My head rests upon his bosom. My burdens, my anguish, my loneliness I leave among the lilies. Ecstasy in the arms of the Beloved, the one who calls me Beloved. (*There is no greater joy than you,* I pray and feel kneeling on the hardwood floor of my pink adolescent bedroom.) Only now can I call night—that lonely dark—lovely and guiding, as St. John of the Cross does. It is the night that unites "Beloved with lover, Lover transformed in the Beloved."[20]

*

Always, there is that hidden room up the secret ladder. There is the cleft in the rock, the hiding place, the garden. There is the cool quiet in the shadow of divine wings. There is a space for my weary head under the crook of God's neck. When I am alone down here on the ground, I can be at the same moment within a sanctum of intimacy. Out of the most profound emptying, God opens Godself as a dwelling place.

*

Perhaps on cold and lonely days I weep because my sense of belonging is misplaced. Though made for infinity, I think I can fit myself here in this blink of space and time. So I exchange a tent for a home in hardwood and plaster. I stack my pennies high as if bank accounts were eternal. I do not say the true and offensive words I must say because I fear a rejecting palm. But I—pilgrim, stranger, alien, other—am called towards a country I cannot see. I am bound in communion with a being I cannot touch.

I belong, I belong, at the deepest roots of my being, I belong.

But it is not here.

*

And yet. In kindergarten, when I first learned what loneliness was, a little red-headed girl named Mimi gave me a ring. It was a cheap, gold-plated thing, a chip of plastic amber set between two faux diamond chips. I do not have any other memories of her or know the rest of her story. But I do remember that I named my red-headed Cabbage Patch doll "Mimi" and keep the ring in a little pink jewelry-box drawer to this day.

*

What if spiritual ecstasy is not enough? What do I do with my longings to know other human beings, my hungering to be close to them (and closest to my husband, despite the bones in the way)? If every Christian is part of my own body, if I am part of every other Christian body, why do I feel so separate? If I need others to become who I am meant to be, why does so much of my life seem to follow a solitary path? How do I constantly move magnetized to people even as they repel me?

*

Perhaps this, the place of questions, is precisely where I'm meant to rest awhile. In *The Great Belonging*, spiritual director Charlotte Donlon encourages the lonely to develop a curious posture towards the grace of loneliness, approaching it not as something to be fixed, but as a companion to whom to listen.[21] She writes, "When loneliness shows up like a scruffy neighborhood cat begging for attention, I can give it a bowl of milk and be curious. Where might it have come from? What feeds its hunger? What does it ask of me right now?"[22]

I open my journal and write.

*

To be welcomed inside, I must first be outside. To be filled, I must first be hungry. To know the sweetness of divine communion, poet George Herbert's Love who invites the guilty to eat at her table and is surely redolent of Chanel, I must first know the taste of loneliness.[23] Only then can I begin to understand, and give, grace.

*

And I must know my loneliness at its keenest point: the darkness that separated Jesus from his Father on the cross, that separates me from my holy Father. This dark is not the midnight dark of intimacy, but the lightless void of self-obsession. Knowing the depths of my own internal darkness—the self-pity, the pride, the refusal to see the universe in others—humbles. And humility opens my hands to receive divine grace and to be a little Christ, embody hospitable Love.

*

It is winter and soon to be dark. My husband and I are preparing a table for guests. We have uprooted ourselves again from Ethiopia and returned to the US. My old friends have become strangers. My old church home is no longer home. We are trying to plant ourselves again.

As my mother taught me, I center each fork over a folded paper napkin. Her recipe for crock-pot roast and potatoes now imbues the house with a savory fragrance. I embody how she snaps a match against its box and lights a candle. Perhaps I spritz my wrists with a hint of Chanel.

Everything I give I have received.

*

After we close the door behind our guests, weariness re-leases itself all over my body. My feet begin to ache and my muscles tremble from flitting back and forth from kitchen to table and back again. I have only a measured portion of energy to give before I stumble into bitter fatigue. Before I begin to burrow into myself again, shut the door tight.

Weary, I climb the secret ladder, crumple my body within the divine lap. Like a weaned child with her mother, I am calm and quiet in the dark. And, for a moment, this being held is enough.

culled salt:

on saying goodbye

Two prisoners whose cells adjoin communicate with each other by knocking on the wall. The wall is the thing which separates them, but it is also their means of communication. It is the same with us with God; every separation is a link.

—Simone Weil, Gravity and Grace

And when your sorrow is comforted (time soothes all sorrows) you will be content that you have known me.

—Antoine de Saint-Exupéry, The Little Prince

It is rainy season in Addis Ababa. Evening clouds gather, soon to heap rain on the roofs. Kaki has wrapped her hair in a scarf, her worn-out body in a bathrobe. After laboring as CFO of a multi-million-*birr* company, she returns to manage her home: supervising Aster the house-helper, stirring *wat* over the electric burner, nurturing plants that grew up with her two boys, one of whom is my husband. In this rare moment, she rests on the family-room couch, head propped by her fist. "When I was young," she says, "Nobody moved."

Wrapped in a fleece blanket on the adjacent loveseat, I listen. I know she is speaking of Dagi and me. We left our life in Addis to pursue graduate school in the US, but returned some days ago for a visit. It has been two years. In the dim quiet, I observe Kaki's face, those eyes full of stories. Lids rise revealing caves, and inside I can see the shadows of nights spent praying alone, hollowed days loud with echoes. She is trying to express this, the heft of a mother's suffering.

"When the sons got married, they lived with their wives in their parents' homes. Everyone was always together." Kaki is perhaps speaking of her rural hometown in southern Ethiopia, opening a page of her story, so gently. I have never spoken with her in such an intimate way, didn't even know her English was this good. For the first time, I am realizing myself as daughter, her as mother. Did I have to leave first to experience this kind of intimacy? When Dagi and I lived just a ten-minute drive away, had we been too shy? Or maybe the moment had not been right? Absence changes things: when you return, you see what routine hid from your eyes. You are shaken, broken from cycles.

I see. I am shaken, broken.

"It was better that way," Kaki continues, and her eyes seek their edges. She does not speak with a sense of accusation or bitterness. When my own mother thinks of Kaki and how much she misses her son, tears glass her eyes, and for a few moments she cannot speak. Now we gather around a flicker of time together in Dagi's childhood home, sharing bowls of savory *shiro*, talking, really talking, for the first time. The time is never enough.

In the lost world Kaki speaks of, she would be content. But as a daughter, I would have had to leave my father's home. I would have been uprooted, like Kaki herself. As a girl, she left her hometown for opportunities in the capital, married a local engineer, and created a little haven hidden from the chaotic streets, a garden. Kaki's Protestant faith also distinguishes her from her Orthodox family, though she hasn't suffered the closed doors, the thrown stones many Ethiopian evangelicals have. She speaks the language of her hometown rarely, maybe during family visits, weddings, or funerals. Either Kaki or her family must take the four-hour bus ride from the southern town to the northern capital. In the dogged pursuit of intimacy, someone always has to be uprooted.

As people straddling two continents, Dagi and I have uprootings grounded deeply into our heart-soil. They never get any easier. The first time Dagi traveled with me to America was for our wedding—the wedding his mother would attempt to obtain a visa for and fail, a challenge his friends, father, and brother would not even try, because what is the point when you are an Ethiopian seeking to enter the Disneyland of America? The night we left was cold and rain splattered the stones.

The house-helper Kidist (her name means "holy") wept quietly, shadowed against the wall of the house. The little Vitz swallowed our luggage like a grave. When we drove away, I watched Kaki on the porch, her face covered in a red scarf.

*

Dagi's family would later tell us we arrived with the sun. Sun evaporated the rains. The mountain air was warm and damp, and burnt fuel bit our lungs. Leaving the airport, we pushed our leaning skyscrapers of luggage down the ramps to the parking lot, where hundreds of faces gathered, expectant. We were expectant, too, waiting for glimpses of three faces: Dagi's mom, dad, and brother. I wonder why, when I saw my husband embrace his brother Michael, I wanted to weep. And when I embraced Michael myself, how I wanted to weep more. And when I embraced Kaki and Papus, I felt the world going all soft around the corners. Kaki handed me flowers wrapped in red cellophane and would not let go of my hand.

*

At the dinner table, Kaki and I linger over our empty plates, hands still drying. After each meal, we wash our hands, clean fingernails and palms from oil and spice. Aster pours a plastic pitcher of water over our soaped hands, holding a bowl beneath them to catch the sudsy drops. Aster is a young woman who left her family down-country to find work in the big city. She lives in a cell-like room detached from the main house. In the morning I catch her slicing onions by the tubfull. In the evening, she sometimes sits in a corner chair to watch Ethio-TV in the family room. Her smile is illuminating, and rarely disappears.

Tonight perhaps the power has flickered off, and Kaki's face is lit with a solar-powered flashlight hung from the ceiling.

She is speaking of her first-born son. "When Mickey was going to college, I was sad," she said. "He was going far, very far." Aster enters the room and gathers the empty plates, pots, bowls, bag of bread, basket of injera. Maybe she says something to Kaki in Amharic, the language both of them had to learn to travel and work in the capital. They laugh. Aster disappears in silence. "At lunch, I pray in the church," Kaki says. I imagine her in the cool dark, away from the workday clock, away from the streets agog with donkeys, goats, dogs, motorcycles, semis, ancient Toyotas, a confetti of human beings.

Her practice of prayer does not surprise me. She is the kind of woman whose life is defined by separation from self: pressing *gorshas* into her paralyzed mother's lips before she died, refusing to sit while her family eats the labor of her hands, welcoming homeless strangers and family members who wander. One definition of "holy" is "set-apart." The Ethiopian Orthodox church calls its saints *kidus*, the same word for "holy:" set-apart ones.

Light separated from darkness. Salt culled from seawater. For Kaki, separation has become a chosen way of life, a way to life. She continues, "In the church, I would say, 'Why, God?' and cry. One day, I wrote a letter to God." I can hear the clang of slippery dishes in the kitchen, a space detached from the rest of the house to protect the pillows and curtains from smelling of onion and spice and smoke. "I wrote a letter on the ground, with my tears," she said. Kaki's eyes are tired. "After that, I felt better."

*

People in the US ask me if I miss Ethiopia, where I taught for four years, where Dagi grew up, where we passed our first year of marriage. Not much, I think, if I'm honest. I don't miss the overpopulated streets, the bloated busses, the exhaust-blackened oxygen we were forced to breathe. Then I remember the

Alliance Française, which opened to free art exhibitions and jazz concerts. Dagi and I would sit on the stone steps in the courtyard, that cultivated garden under the stars. At the end of the night after the musicians had clicked their instruments into their cases, we would laugh in each other's arms until deep in the night. (The night depths are not all for tears).

Of course, missing family is a given.

*

It hit me at the rehearsal the night before our wedding. A round of stained glass colored the chapel green and garnet. I wore my curly hair long and wild. I was flaunting my last day of singleness, perhaps, in my loosed curls. The whole routine clicked into place, until my dad and I stood at the beginning of the aisle, and he took my hand. He was taking my hand to let it go again. He would let it go at the end of the aisle, where my almost-husband stood. Let go: my rose room on the second-floor of my parents' home (strange to say "my parents'" home now, no longer mine), my mom's homemade chicken and dumplings, my known role of unmarried daughter. Suddenly my whole body shook with convulsions rising from some abyss swiftly opened beneath my sandals. In a second, everything became real as my trembling fingers.

Union requires separation, and marriage requires separation of that intensely breaking kind. Sometimes it seems the mind is the last to understand what is happening. It was only when my body started trembling that I realized marriage was far more profound than I had ever imagined.

A long-time family friend once spoke about life after his eldest daughter married and left the house—a neat, white bungalow under shady trees on Elbert Street. He said he missed the trails she left in the house when she returned at the end of each day: her shoes by the door, an empty plate at the table, a book left on the loveseat. All signs she was still there, still present. Life stirred. And then after the wedding, after she left was like after a funeral. Like a death in the family.

Is this how my mother feels, how Kaki feels, when their children leave home? It is a feeling I cannot fully comprehend. I have always been the one leaving for new adventures, not the one left grieving in an emptied house. When I left the US for Ethiopia as a recent university-grad, my gut ached with missing, but it was a missing quickly filled with the rewarding labor of learning the culture, meeting people from around the world, teaching classrooms full of quivering souls. Those I left behind remained locked in the old routines with nothing new to fill the gaping of a loved presence. There were nights in Addis I lay on damp pillows listening to the music my dad would play at home. The loss felt like a physical ailment. Loss is a physical ailment. But my mother's aching, Kaki's aching, is different. "It is hard, very hard," Kaki said once (or was it more than once?). She is an Ethiopian woman, and Ethiopians press their emotions under radiant smiles, hidden under the weight of the day's labors and incantations of "Thanks be to God."

I do not know my own mother's private aches, what she says to God when the door of her room is closed, but I can tell you what I do see. When I arrive in Indianapolis from Ethiopia and see my arthritic mother at the end of the terminal, she is always jumping up and down, up and down holding a poster board decorated in hearts and rows of exclamation points. When I reach her, she holds me in her strong arms, tight, and that's when she always breaks down.

*

One of my favorite pictures of our wedding glimpses Dagi and me dancing on the grass in the summer gloaming. The photograph was taken after the father-daughter dance, when my dad and I swayed to the song he chose: Billy Joel's "Lullaby." It was taken after my father released my hand and my hand wove into my new husband's. Dagi's smile is pressed into my ear, and my face is turned away from the camera. I am resting my face on his shoulder. Dried lavender clings to my hair, from that moment our dear guests pelted us with handfuls of the fragrant buds as we emerged from the church, husband and wife, walking into the world for the first time as a new kind of one. My curls unwind down the white buttons of my dress, where Dagi's hand rests. He was whispering the lyrics of the song, a rap song. Our rings sit bright on our fingers. Here are the words that speak when I remember that moment: *And God saw everything he had made, and behold, it was very good.*[1]

*

Creation demands separation. It surprises me how often the word "separate" is used in the first chapter of Genesis. *God separated the light from the darkness*, and, *God said, 'Let there be an expanse in the midst of the waters, and let it separate the waters from the waters,'* and, *'Let there be lights in the expanse of the heavens to separate the day from the night.'* Separation creates the order requisite for life. Light is birthed in its divorce from chaos.

At the end of the wedding, after embracing our beloveds, Dagi and I drove away in my mom's little red MG, headlights burrowing a path through back country roads.

*

About a year ago, my sister gave the universe a new life. She wrestled for nearly twenty-four hours to birth her son, that is, to separate her body from his. In the end, we gathered around the hospital room and rubbed antiseptic foam on our hands and held this fragile and glorious being. Fluorescent light divided womb dark. One of my sisters wept. His name is Moses. Moses, drawn from the Nile waters. Separated from his family to lead a nation into the Promised Land.

*

If separation is requisite for life, for the stunning emergence of monarch wings, it also lies at the origin of death. After the bitten fruit and the shifted blame, Adam and Eve become self-conscious of their naked bodies, their vulnerable intimacy. The divine garden walks shuttered. A holy cherubim wielding a sword of flame bars the path to Paradise. Medieval monk Anselm of Canterbury expresses the state of humanity in his *Proslogion*:

> Wretched, expelled from that home, impelled to this one! Cast down from that abode, sunken to this one! From our homeland into exile, from the vision of God into our own blindness, from the delight of immortality into the bitterness and horror of death. O miserable transformation from such great good into such great evil! What a grievous loss, a heavy sorrow, an unmitigated plight![2]

*

While in Addis for our visit, I have no work or television or phone. In between time with family and friends—joking with Kaki, watching a video of a friend hang-gliding on her Brazilian honeymoon (She is an Ethiopian who left her family in Addis to live down-country with her Dutch husband), spooning bowls of bean soup, sipping tea by the window, all beautiful sources of nourishment—I read. I am reading Dr. Martin Luther King Jr.'s "Letter from a Birmingham Jail" for the first time. Dagi and I talk often about racism. Marriage, that stunning oneness, has given us the gift of wearing each other's skins in a way. To see life intimately alongside—however imperfectly—the eyes of a black man has shredded my white paper world. The whole letter burns, but one passage flew like a spark. Speaking of segregation, Dr. King writes,

"Paul Tillich has said that sin is separation. Is not segregation an existential expression of man's tragic separation, his awful estrangement, his terrible sinfulness?"[3]

Anselm nods from his damp cell in medieval Caen.

Segregation still splinters my hometown. Neighborhoods, schools. Even churches remain divided. "Don't talk about racism," certain white evangelicals complained at a recent conference in the Midwest, after a pastor had just given a talk on the subject. "Let's get back to the Bible."

Sin as separation.

Separation as segregation.

Segregation as sin.

Is this partly why saying goodbye is so hard? Like sin, like segregation, like any kind of death, leaving a beloved feels wrong, as if it is not meant to be. Sometimes I wonder if we were meant to live like Kaki's people down-country, like people across the world lived for ages: never leaving. Husbands never leaving their mothers. Mothers never having to suffer without their sons. The wives leaving, but only once. (The move was painful, but quick.) We were meant to live in close community, a sweet intimacy. We were meant to live always in a garden where everything was green and good.

Or is it that the pain of separation is merely a metaphor for the pain evil causes? *Against you, you only, have I sinned*, cries David, who clove a man from his wife and clove the man from his own breath.[4] Union (Bathsheba spied from the rooftop, gathered from her cleansing) demands separation, and in this tragedy, the separation horrifies. Even the life born of the oneness was lost. When I look at another man too long, there is a tear rent not only between my husband and me, but between God and me. Perhaps I do not feel the pain in the moment, but when I understand my action as it is—the abyss opened and my body shook—I mourn as if for a loss, a separation, a kind of death. The metaphor seems apt when I remember Kaki's red scarf the night her son left for a wedding across the sea.

Police Commissioner "Bull" Connor arrested Dr. King in Birmingham on Good Friday. On Good Friday, Christ cried, *My God, my God, why have you forsaken me?*[5] Christ knew separation: from heaven, from Mary's body, from the crowds, from his disciples, now from a holy God who cannot abide the heft of humanity's evil heavy on his Son. Perfect Trinitarian intimacy broken for the first time in the ages. Under a dark sky, Mary weeps. Christ, holding his mother's heart, holding all mothers' hearts, gives her into John's care, him into hers.

In the end, this separation is a grace. Through it, humans enter the Holy of Holies, iron veil torn from ceiling to hem. Humans can be bound again with the divine. Believers are given the call to live as aliens on this planet, as holy ones, set-apart-ones, salted and shook with light.

We dream again of walking with God in the garden.

*

One night at the parking lot of Igloo, a new ice cream parlor with cherry-red tables and the best brownie sundae you can find in Addis, I weep for the first time saying goodbye to Dagi's friends. This surprises me. They had always been Dagi's friends, not mine, but during our visit I have learned to love them as I never had when we lived here. Routine waters down the transcendence, the grave import of moments. There is nothing like leaving and returning to help you see how things are. G.K. Chesterton: "There are two ways of getting home; and one of them is to stay there. The other is to walk round the whole world till we come back to the same place."[6]

We had to come back to Addis to see what it was.

I feel this over and over again, as the end of our time in Ethiopia approaches, as we say goodbye again and again: *Goodbye Kaki, Papus, Mickey, Fevi, Liron, Aster, Kaleb, Frezer, Agazite, Samir, Marut, Mark, Taffy, Chimon, Josiah, Temesgen, Tsega, Jo, Medan, Kathy, Brett, Heeyon, Theresa, Aki, Deborah, Joy, Chris,*

Erin, Kate, Yvonne, Schlitz, AJ, Lydia, Zewdu, Ruth, Tsihiy, Girma, Eteye Mihiret . . .

Each goodbye is a small death.

Where the living presence was, an emptiness gapes. But the emptiness is something. In Eugene Vodolazkin's novel *Laurus*, in which holy fool Arseny travels the known world in an epic journey ending at the place of his birth, Brother Hugo wonders if it is worth getting to know someone if you must say goodbye later. Arseny replies, "There is emptiness before meeting someone, just nothing, but there is no longer emptiness after parting. After having met someone once, it is impossible to part completely."[7]

The ache is something.

*

We fly from Ethiopian heights and return to Midwestern flatlands. Here I tend a garden where daisies grow. (The daisies are transplants from my grandmother.) I fill jars with their abundance and give them away. Here we enjoy slow Sunday brunches with my parents at their brick farmhouse, the only house set sideways on the street. Here my mother embraces us with every joy Dagi's mother felt the days we passed in her presence.

We leave one world and unite with another. We break and heal. The breaking is necessary for the healings, and our healed hearts must be broken again. Sometimes I cannot stand the limitations of my own skin. I wish I could rend the barriers of time and place and be with everyone all at once, a gift reserved (blessedly, in the end) for God.

I suppose the best I can do is to be alive and aware wherever I am.

*

After my first year of living in Ethiopia, before I met Dagi, returning to America felt like a wound un-healing, going back in time. My room felt claustrophobic. Home did not feel like home. Hair bound in Ethiopian braids, an Orthodox cross about my neck, I even wrestled with my own identity as an American. No one understood. Desperate to find someone who would, I met with one of my sister's friends in a chain coffee shop where the air conditioner was too cold and the service too fast. My sister's friend had lived a year in Thailand. Our conversation was balm.

"You know," she said. "It's hard having your heart in two places."

"Makes me long for heaven," I said.

I think of that great severance from earthly life, being born, really born, for the first time. I imagine Kaki and my mom together in that place of light, that wedding feast. Their eyes seem to glow because they will not have to say goodbye ever again.

"Yes," she said, and her eyes brightened with a kind of longing. "Someday we will be with everyone, all together." She looked away.

Part Two: Stasis

the blissful abyss:

on boredom

All of humanity's problems stem from man's inability to sit quietly in a room alone.

—Blaise Pascal, Pensées

Might we consider boredom as not only necessary for our life but also as one of its greatest blessings? A gift, pure and simple, a precious chance to be alone with our thoughts and alone with God?

—Kathleen Norris, Acedia and Me

1. Be happy about it.

If you find yourself in that happy state of boredom, count yourself blessed. It is a gift to be bored, because being bored means you have seen through the frippery and gauze of the world's distractions.

Binge-watching TV, you realize, is like eating buckets of cotton candy, but for your soul. You find yourself not sated, but hungrier in spirit than when you started, sugar-diving into depression after swallowing half a strawberry cake. You feel let down, like you'd expected a filet mignon, but the server brought a Big Mac. This is good. Elucidating. Freeing. Disillusionment can be a gift, like finally finding a pair of eyeglasses that work.

Or maybe you prefer books. (I'm not leaving us book snobs out of this.) You think you are better than the TV-bingers, but you are just as bad, consuming not images, but words. Both books and shows can boil down to distractions. Most pop fiction aside, books can sometimes seem more sophisticated: delving into "meaningful" topics such as existentialism and socialism and minimalism. True, these ideas may make you more informed (soap operas are notoriously silent on the subject of economics), may help you to become "a better version of yourself." But information and self-help are meaningless without a deep kind of soul transformation. Without love, as St. Paul wrote, you're just banging pots and pans around.[1]

Or, perhaps you are literary, seeking in books the elusive, universal Beauty whose lover is burly Truth. An admirable aim. But how much does your desire for what is "higher" merely lead you into a devious, hidden kind of puffy-feathered pride, all the more noxious for the suit of sophistication it wears? (I know; I've got my own downy costume.)

Anything else you may try to distract yourself with—drinking, eating, dancing, gaming, email-checking, conference-calling, discussing, cooking, gardening, cleaning, body-building, running, running, running—you've found lacking in some way. No matter how noble or what they call "good for you," everything eventually dissolves to sand in the bottom of the hourglass. You've found that most clarifying of truths: nothing under the sun is enough.[2]

Like I said, this is good.

2. Avoid making a to-do list.

You thought this article would be a list of activities. Like:

1. Learn to play "House of the Rising Sun" on the guitar hiding in a slim cloak of dust in the spare room.
2. If tackling the first, buy a pair of noise-canceling headphones for those you live with.
3. Take a meditative walk in a nearby nature preserve.
4. Bake cupcakes from scratch.
5. Watch YouTube videos on perfecting your French accent.
6. Call your mom.
7. Plant an herb garden.
8. Clean out the fridge.
9. Try a new flavor of jelly bean.
10. Draw a tree.

None of these actions are bad or wrong. All of them can be creative ways of using your time. But to give you a list like this, at this most propitious and pregnant point of boredom, would be only to stick a Band-Aid over your wound. For this itchiness, this restlessness in the face of that great hollow space of boredom is symptomatic of a deeper reality, a kind of bruising or illness or burn.

If you were to make another list, you'd destroy this beautiful chance you're being given. You'd just continue spinning, spinning on that ceaseless wheel, hounded by that nebulous, self-constructed pressure to do. It wouldn't stop until you wheeled yourself into your tombstone.

Resist the urge to rush past into another activity, another distraction, another flashing mirror.

Take off your coat, stay awhile.

Because boredom is a gift. It's a gift to arrive here before this chasm, this void full of potentialities. It takes some effort and time to have wandered to this most enigmatic and eloquent, grandest of canyons. To have seen through the moguls' conspiracy to entrap its inhabitants in the viny tentacles of absolute, continuous, infinite entertainment. (Scroll, scroll, scroll—it does not end.) You've burned one of the veils, and this is good.

Not everyone receives the grace to reach here.

3. Let go.

All day long you've been picking distractions like half-price pints at a blueberry farm. First, it was the alarm clock, that racket hammering your sweet dreams to pieces. Then after recovering from that shock, checking the weather app on your phone to see what to wear. It's impossible just to check one app because the phone is a metamorphosing demon with a hundred hands, grabbing. In a few seconds, you've checked your work email, your personal email, your Insta account, the morning's headlines, and laughed at a funny meme—having completely forgotten to see what the weather would be today. You've returned to the black box of death, full of tussling Sirens. You narrowly emerged with enough time to scarf down breakfast and scuttle through the door.

And this is just the morning, before the real problems started: like avoiding chatty colleagues and how you completely forgot about that meeting and what to make for dinner and the rest of that to-do list spiraling off your desk into oblivion.

But you're here now. Bored as a dead rat, as the French say. Good.

Now let it all go.

Let go: the suffocating stacks of information your brain is insufficient to bear. Let go: how that lady cut you off and how you spilled tea on your new-bleached sleeve. Let go: the ceaseless sputterings they call news. Let go: the tense cats fighting in your shoulders and right down through your back. Let go: the wonderful lines in that book you read. Let go: the insightful podcast and the jazz slipping through the radio. Let go: what you need to remember. Let go: what you forgot. Let go: that impulse, that thought.

Let it go.

Everything.

Until all you hold is nothing.

4. Feel.

Now that you are here and happy(ish), you can open yourself to that most tumultuous of internal spaces: emotions. At the risk of impersonating a therapist, let the feelings rise and swirl around.

What appears?

Before continuing, just a word of warning: it's very likely you'll wish to armor yourself in your hiking boots and stamp the feelings back into the mysterious ether from which they slipped. They are unruly, yes, and sometimes redolent with the scent of unburied bones. Perhaps this emotions-smothering has been a habit. Stamp the habit instead.

As you stand before the widening gape of nothingness threatening to engulf you, perhaps one feeling that arises is that aforementioned itch. The itch to do something. Anything. Right now. Perhaps it's the itch to grasp something solid, because the bastions you structure your life around—doing everything on the to-do list, say, and doing it as if your mother were to inspect it—have suddenly given way, dissolved like sugar cubes in boiling tea. All those tasks that form your life's meaning shift to shallowness.

Maybe it's the amorphous antimatter of despair as you mourn the fact that nothing will satisfy here where the grass grows. Nothing will be enough. You've tried everything, every distraction.

But nothing fills you—and that notion terrifies.

And now arises that hateful crone crying that you are worthless. Confession: I often confuse what I do with who I am. If I wash the dishes, do the laundry, and whip up a home-made dinner by six, I am worth something. If I read a literary book and have some "deep" thoughts on it (having overcome the scandalous desire to wander around in a British mystery novel instead), I feel sophisticated, better than. If I am kind to my husband and call my grandparents just to say hi, I am a good person. Because I do all this, I am worth the oxygen I breathe, the shoe print I press into the ecosystem. I am worth loving.

But when my doings are taken away, when it is just me existing, without all of the achievements I hide behind, stand upon, eat as bread—when it is just me, I feel so naked, vulnerable, worthless.[3]

Who am I without what I do?

Then comes the red pan-crasher called fear. It's like when I haven't eaten in hours and my blood sugar plummets: this sudden smack of what feels like a life-threatening emptiness. I need something. Quick. Inject me with a sugar rush of Insta or a poem or a headline. There's a sense of panic, like I've just been cut off from oxygen.

But it's all good, this hungry void. Don't worry. Like fasting, this emptiness can lead you to something that will actually satisfy.

5. Listen.

If you're a journaler or a diarist, you could get out your tea-and-tear-splattered volume penned in the darker moments. If you're not, that's okay. Try to listen.

Beware: what you hear may not be easy.

When you listen in the void, realities begin to arise from despair's abyss (if you are anything like me). When you take a moment to pause, you allow yourself to realize some things. After visiting my parents as my Grandpa lay dying, this thought struck: *I probably should've listened to my dad finish his meaningful thought, before I abruptly left the conversation to help my mom make the bed. I bet he felt bad about that.* Or, *I haven't called my Nana in weeks, or months. I'm sure she is lonely and would appreciate a call.* Or, *When was the last time I prayed, not to air an unending list of wants—but just to listen?*

You may hear some things you've needed to hear for a long time. And the things may hurt. But it's a good hurt, a hurt that leads to healing.

Sometimes even the big questions, those unanswerable ones, begin to circulate like Furies. "Why am I here on this earth?" and "What have I been doing with my life all these years?" and "I am old. Look at these gray hairs springing from my skull. Not much time left to do what I need to do. What is it that I need to do?"

It's hard, I know. (I am with you, here.) But allow these questions to rise, to shove past the layers of movies and magazines and muffins that you've carefully constructed to paper over what really matters.

What really matters?

Or you may hear nothing. That's okay, great even. It could be that hearing nothing is just what you need to hear. Just enjoy the emptiness. Enjoy the space to breathe, the companionable silence of God.

Or perhaps you just need to practice boredom more. Allow more space in your life that's not jammed with tweets and twits and twangs. After finishing a movie, giving a few moments for pondering. When you're standing in a long checkout line, observing the demeanor of the cashier and preparing a kind word to say. When you're stuck in a waiting room, orienting your heart heavenward.

You might need to practice boredom like you'd practice meditation or prayer. Boredom as spiritual practice. Holy boredom.

6. Practice dying.

When you die, you'll experience the emptiness of every earthly thing: no more holding sun rays in your fingers, no more wine to *seeswirlsipswishspit*. My dying Grandpa doesn't wish for more afternoons in Judge Judy's courtroom or for more candy bars (like the time I snuck a bag bought from the gas station into his room at the rehab center and he gobbled them with glee). Here, at the precipice of existence, it seems he has found all things lacking.

Perhaps boredom could be a way of practicing for death, then. And not just dead death, the funeral kind. Self-death, the cross-bearing kind. It's a good practice to pause before the demands of instant satiation: the finger hovering over the click, the spoon held before the lips, the split second between the glimpse and the heart-shift to lust.

It's good to stop, to question that next impulse to seek and do and stock yourself with *moremoremore*. It's good to make a habit of arresting those appetites, whatever kind they may be. As St. James says, desire conceived leads to sin; and sin with legs leads to death.[4] Some desires are better left dead.

In this way, you will not be ruled by them. When you refuse to give into all your desires, you become their ruler. You ascend to a kind of control. A kind of transcendence happens. You are better poised now for what you are made for, and who you are.

Beyond desire, you reach an open space. It's freeing. Unfettered from the demands of wantings and desirings, you are liberated.

Where will you fly?

7. Be led.

You're waiting, winged, paused. Desires rest at your feet, like somniferous kittens. The questions and feelings have arisen from the vaporous void and you've had coffee with them. You've let silence unload your heart. You've set aside your muscular and pushy will.

What now?

That I cannot say. It is different for each person. God has something different to whisper to each pair of ears alone. Intimate as a secret.

But I do know the sense of being led. A sense of waiting, crouched in the corner, eyes at the master's fingers: attending the next step.[5]

vanished flights and snow days:

on cancellations

The beauty of the world appears when we recognize that the substance of the universe is necessity and that the substance of necessity is obedience to a perfectly wise Love.

—Simone Weil, The Love of God and Affliction

Whatever happens. Whatever
what is is is what
I want. Only that. But that.

—Galway Kinnell, "Prayer"

God willing.

The words always gave me pause. As a fresh college graduate teaching in Ethiopia, I had never before heard them so often expressed. They seemed to question, though not in a defeatist or fatalistic sense, that plans would actually happen. Whether it was after organizing an outing for later that week or a vacation for later that year, Ethiopians would consistently qualify their plans with "God willing."

"We'll visit the lake this summer, God willing."

"Meet you for coffee next week, God willing."

"See you at home tonight, God willing."

In Ethiopia, people tend to live in greater conscious dependence on God than the Americans I know. The presence of faith infuses the culture: the Orthodox fast from animal products 208 days of the year; mosques sound the call to prayer across the land five times a day; and the evangelical Protestant church next door to the school where I taught flooded with the faithful in exuberant worship services multiple times a week.[1] Traditional greetings—exchanged between everyone from colleagues at the office to friends grabbing coffee—praise God for health, family, work. In a country where 90% of the population lives on less than $5.50 a day, daily dependence on God is a lived reality.[2] No wonder plans acknowledge God as the One who ultimately holds them and decides if they will come to pass, or not:

Endeg egzhabihair fekad.
Inch'allah.
God willing.

*

Born and raised in middle-class America, I was not accustomed to canceled plans. Most of what I had planned, happened: learning the classical guitar, running a mile, completing a college degree. I had heard the Christian cliché, "Write your plans in pencil; God holds the eraser," but couldn't validate it with personal experience.

Even now looking at American culture, I see how our prized sense of boisterous confidence, our money (or imaginary money, i.e. credit), and our capacity to grant ourselves almost any imaginable wish instantaneously give us a heady illusion of power and control. A few clicks can bring dinner or door hinges or a date. I seem to think that everything in life will be just as easy.

When things don't go according to plan (a canceled flight or a snow day), I too often consider it an aberrance. I am baffled that nature or events (or God?) would so conspire to ruin my highly developed, risk-proofed plans. After my momentary confusion, rather than learning from this glimpse of my own impotence, rather than pausing, humbled, I rush to plan my next activity with renewed vigor. Must've been a kink in the system, I shrug.

*

In the spring of 2020 when the COVID pandemic shuttered the globe, I was, in the words of a friend's text, "shook." The breadth of canceled events was unprecedented: professional sports leagues, conferences, concert tours, flights. Each day the severity of the cancellations intensified: the public library, restaurants and bars, all non-essential businesses, and, closest to home for my husband and me, school and church until May at least.

With fear and trembling, I booked a ticket to visit my sisters in Denver, but held it loosely. "Hope to see you in just a couple of weeks," I texted them, and, for one of the first times in my life, I qualified the phrase with "God willing."

The words were a kind of prayer, a way of praying without cessation.[3] They opened an essential dimension to my plans, orienting them heavenward. And they invited God into the daily weave of my plan-making. Into the grit and bone of life. Perhaps this is part of the gift of cancellations: learning to say, or rather, pray, with conviction, "May this be, God willing."

*

Though at times unsettling, there can be something thrilling in the unexpected, the sudden openness loosed in canceled plans. The winter before the world shut down, my husband and I were driving to the airport from a wedding in balmy Orlando, when we got a text. "Our flight is canceled!" I announced with elation. Snow had snuffed our city—including its airport—in impenetrable white.

"Are you serious?" my husband said. He could think only of the annoyance of missing our flight, missing work the next day, finding a hotel and rental car. I could think only of the excitement of missing our flight, missing work the next day, finding a hotel and rental car. In the end, we slept one more night in Orlando at the cheapest hotel we could find. The next morning, I sipped coffee by the lonely pool, letting the Floridian sun seep deep into my pores before returning to blizzard-bound Indianapolis.

Months later, the moment the head of school announced the pandemic would cancel classes for the next three weeks (how little we knew how long the cessation of normalcy would really be), my French I students exploded from their seats and punched their hands in the air and danced just quietly enough to hear the rest of the announcement. When the PA clicked off, the school volcanized in huzzahs. Many thanked God that they didn't have to take their midterms (and I was thanking him that I wouldn't have to grade them). My mom, positive as usual in moving with life's undulations, texted our family's thread: "It's like a movie!" Upon which one of my younger sisters sent a GIF from Hitchcock's *Birds*.

Weeks later when the whole globe became homebound, as if gripped in an apocalyptic blizzard, my husband and I took the government's stay-at-home orders with a measure of glee. As introverted introverts, we envisioned hours reading or watching movies with bowls of ice cream at hand. Finally, I would have time for all those things I'd shelved: baking baguettes, planting a vegetable garden, cleaning out the refrigerator, writing that book (all of which I did). Being forced to stay home would free us from societal constraints to be somewhere and do something. Like children, we would be liberated to move with our whims. One of my friends said (and this was in the honeymoon of our confinement), "It's like the whole world is having a snow day."

One of the best things about childhood snow days was their surprise. In the morning dark, my mom would pad into the room I shared with my siblings and whisper, "School is canceled!" I would arise with elation. Suddenly, the hours were freed from bells and straight pencils and desk-confinement to scampering in the snow and watching TV and sipping homemade hot chocolate in fresh, dry socks.

Even now, I love a good snow. Like writer Katherine May, "I love the inconvenience the same way that I sneakingly love a bad cold: the irresistible disruption to mundane life, forcing you to stop for a while and step outside your normal habits."[4] The ordinary is vanquished, routines suspended. Possibilities glitter.

More often than not, I feel relief when plans are canceled. Though as I get older and realize the difficulty of coordinating plans with other continually-occupied adults, I still feel something break loose, unconstrict in my chest when plans fall through. Somehow, life seems freer, untied from schedules and organized play. Somehow, seeing the truth of my own limitations is oddly comforting: for a moment, I realize I do not bear the heft of the world.

*

Granted, a government-mandated lockdown embodies the opposite of liberation: invisible bars over the windows and doors. Just one week into "social distancing," I (the biggest introvert I know) started to feel the constriction of the times deep within my ribcage. Quarantine permits a measure of whim-granting—but only within the walls of home. TV-watching and ice-cream-eating and Amazon-buying wear after a while.

Like any creative act, making plans—meeting for coffee, jiving to a jazz band, or munching pretzels at a ball game—is an expression of freedom. Part of the gift of cancellations is learning to be grateful that God gives the grace to make plans at all. That God graciously allows our designs to take shape at all. That God gives us the gift of community at all. A gathering with friends is a small miracle, one that calls for gratitude.

The complexity of steps that must be orchestrated for a simple dinner party is fathomless. Overloaded schedules must sync. Each invited body must be healthy, carefully protected from common colds and more unusual maladies of broken bones and viruses, stomach bugs and disease. And who can fathom the immune system's invisible labor: countless battles between white blood cells and invading germs, all unseen?

Grocery stores must carry the chicken and pasta and greens and wine and all the fixings for apple crumble. Which means that planes and trucks and pilots and drivers had to be in good working order to deliver the fresh food on time. Faithful farmers had to tend the greens, the wheat, the apples for long months: each season, each week, each day, demanding a particular rhythm of care. The chicken had to emerge from shell and eat and grow and be slaughtered.

And this is not to mention the realms beyond the grip of human hands: the precise ratio of sun and rain, heat and cold necessary for greens and chickens to thrive. The unseen labors of root, stem, and bud: osmosis opening pores on the undersides of leaves, photosynthesis transforming sunlight into sugar. The microscopic organisms smelting dead matter into nutrient-rich gold. Even (and especially) the life-giving processes unfolding within the soil are cause for dumbfounded wonder.[5]

*

Several years ago when I was marathoning through my master's degree and full-time teaching job, a canceled small group meeting meant my husband and I could have a thoughtful dinner together, rather than choking down makeshift pizzas (tortillas dashed with mozzarella and tomato sauce from a jar). Forced pauses and emptied hours can give our weary bodies and souls an invitation to the rest we need, but do not regularly enjoy. With any cancellation—school, work, entertainment—we are given a choice: to fight our freedom from labor, or to enjoy cessation as an unexpected gift.

Rest is a rhythm God has sung since the birth of the universe. In the Old Testament, God ordains rest for his people every seventh year[6] and every fiftieth year[7], in addition to seven annual holidays.[8] But the most frequent ritual of rest is the weekly Sabbath.

The noun "Sabbath" seems to be derived from the Hebrew verb *sabat*, which Strong's concordance defines as "to repose, i.e. to desist from exertion . . . cease, cause to cease, let cease, make to cease, celebrate, cause to fail, make to fail, keep, keep Sabbath, suffer to be lacking, leave, put away, put down, rest, make to rest, rid, still, take away."[9] "Cancel" would fit the list quite neatly.

Ironic the extent to which the Hebrew recalls death, death on a day celebrating creation. Cease, fail, put down. Cancel. I conjure morbid images of stilled lungs and failed kidneys and our beloved mutt Patch lying limp across an exam table. "Rest" reminds of eternal rest, a return to dust. What's more, the dying seems intentional: make to cease, cause to fail. To honor the Sabbath, I wonder what must die.

Rhythmic repose is a grave matter. See the divine words burned into stone: *Remember the Sabbath day, to keep it holy.*[10] In the Old Testament, Sabbath-keeping is a litmus test for faithfulness. It is the center, indeed a day of re-centering, from which obedience to divine law comes. Restless laborers beware: the ancient penalty for Sabbath-laborers is death.[11] Prophets warn of divine wrath ignited, poured: Jeremiah presages fire in the gates, palaces devoured in flame.[12] Ezekiel speaks of captivity, a scattering like dandelion seeds.[13] When the Israelites desecrated the Sabbath, God buried them in the wilderness.[14]

What would it be like if the church reverenced the divine call to honor the Sabbath as she did other commandments like *Thou shalt not murder* and *Thou shalt not steal*? Maybe fewer missionaries and pastors would feel guilty canceling work to take vacations, better able to root into the land to which they were called and abide there, rather than quit bitter, beat, burnt out. Fewer church programs could free time for ministry lived organically through daily life: inviting the neighbors over for dinner, sitting with a wounded friend. Before the Flood, before he was immortalized for his insane ark-building scheme, Noah walked with God for five hundred years.[15] If we rested more, we could enjoy more time walking with our Maker, slow like garden strolls.

Rest-refusal marks the faithless. And it marks many of us in the church. Cancellations are perhaps a way of resetting our Sabbath practice. Those who have suddenly unfettered and unclaimed hours hold an opportunity to delight in time with God, with family, with the ones who share our kitchens and bedrooms and living rooms.

*

My father taught me more about the delights of Sabbath rest than anyone. "Balance," he would say with mysterious wisdom, like Mr. Miyagi to Daniel-san. Our post-church Sundays unfolded in naps, drives in the 1967 Jaguar, turning up the music till the walls vibrated. Or we would enjoy a meal at the MCL cafeteria with my Grandpa and return to his trailer to watch TV and snack from his fridge full of Coke and Hershey bars. In the evenings at home, we would eat Papa Murphy's pizza and watch *Monk*. For my dad, Sabbath is more than a Sunday nap. It is a way of living: riding his bike to work like the Dutch or taking his children to lunch or drafting a movie script. All what my dad would call "recreation: Re. Creation."

*

If Sabbath rest acknowledges the spiritual—that I am not merely one who labors, whisking bread crumbs, folding stacks of shirts—it also acknowledges the reality of the body. It is of the greatest encouragement to me that Christ breathed oxygen with human lungs, dust blackening foot crevices, grit under toenails. The phenomenon of the world's redemption unfolded within a frame of flesh.

St. Luke writes, *But Jesus often withdrew to lonely places and prayed.*[16] As a physician, perhaps he attended to Jesus's habits of prayer to offer a picture of embodied spirituality. St. Luke knew, and God knew, the reality of needing: water, bread, rest.

A paradox: the God who needs no rest, who is himself a cool cove of rest offered and given, needed rest. Here, within a skin that sweated and a heart that would cease, resided infinity and all the God-ness of God.[17] Yet Christ emptied himself, not just of heaven, but of endless energy and the ability to literally do it all.[18] (If Christ himself chose not to do it all, how much more should we be free from this arbitrary pressure!)

I cannot comprehend the paradox, but I tremble at such a love.

*

If you do not cancel, cease, make to fail, the body will cancel for you. Overworked Americans have proved this for years, suffering the long-term effects of stress: anxiety, depression, burnout, chronic fatigue, insomnia, forgetfulness, dizziness, headaches, chest pain, shortness of breath, acne.[19] Our unused vacation days and twenty-four-seven service have left us one of the most depressed nations in the world.[20]

I proved this truth in my own body. Years ago after planning two weddings on two different continents while teaching full time in Ethiopia, after the fervid celebrations, the shocking sudden oneness that is marriage, after the honeymoon in a lonely cottage by the Albemarle Sound, my body collapsed. I could barely walk to the mailbox, and wrote to the mission school saying I wasn't sure if I could return the next academic year. My new husband and I visited doctors; grave white coats conducted tests for parasites, anemia, malaria, mononucleosis. Nothing. The verdict, not diagnosed, but puzzled together: exhaustion.

*

The other day, I was reading in *Modern Agriculture* about farmers in British Columbia who allow valuable fields to lie fallow, sometimes for four or more years. "Local research has shown that growing these crops continually, year after year, can deplete soil nutrients [and] . . . may also lead to degradation of soil structure."[21] Giving the fields rest also allows for the recreation (re. creation) of the local habitat: burrowing owl, microbats, mottled duskywing. Hidden life appears. Pause and rest allow a world to awaken.

Earth unreleased to cease shifts to dust. Scientists warn of millions of US acres crumbling into sand due to pressures to produce more, more.[22] Burdened farmers beat corn out of the soil, wearing it out, weary. The land tires, slips away into streams. Disappears. And with it the ability to produce food, to house biodiversity, to create and sustain life. A withered branch, thrown into the fire.

Another Dust Bowl. In the 1930s, after generations of over-plowing, dust storms blew away one hundred million acres of the American Great Plains. These "black blizzards" darkened the sun, sometimes for days. Farmers who for decades had refused rest were forced to cancel work, and with them teachers adding sums, mothers chopping onions, toddlers spooning applesauce. After the winds quieted, residents would clear the dust drifts with shovels.[23]

On Black Sunday, the worst blizzard dimmed a sunny day night-dark. A wall of sand and dust whipped up as many as three million acres of topsoil in a storm that lasted hours. Families hid in basements. Drivers hunkered in parked cars. One woman reportedly considered killing her baby to save it from Armageddon.[24]

If American farmers had followed the ancient wisdom in Leviticus, such a calamity might never have happened: *But in the seventh year there shall be a Sabbath of solemn rest for the land, a Sabbath to the LORD. You shall not sow your field or prune your vineyard.*[25] Here God cancels cultivation for a whole year.

Thousands of years before science provided the reasons why, Israelites let their fields lie fallow, an unusual practice in the ancient world. Jews call this year *Shemittah*, "release." Release loans due. Release the right to property and the safety of storing.[26] Release of dependence on self, one's ability to carve a way in the world with wiles and moxie and talent. Release the control of provision: God is the one who places bread in bowls and fills jars with honey, glasses with wine.

Release, falling into the gracious hands of God.

*

Yet, how difficult it can be to release carefully made plans, move gracefully with cancellations outside of our control.

All day, I had prepared a dinner for friends: scrubbing sinks, picking up socks. Chopping potatoes, laying out the silverware. But almost as soon as I pulled the chicken out of the oven, I received an apologetic text canceling our engagement.

Grit appears: complaining about the injustice of labor for (apparently) nothing. Lamenting the chicken growing cold and the beautiful table unlauded. But a small whisper tells me to submit.

Submission.

Submission to what Simone Weil calls "necessity." To different timing. To what I cannot control with my planner or smartphone. To suddenly open hours God allows.

In submission, calming and quieting myself like a child on the breast of a sovereign and good God, I see that unexpected space can be redeemed.[27]

That evening, I packed up half of the dinner and dropped it off with our homebound friends. My husband, son, and I ate a quiet meal together. Was our plan canceled to show me the pride and vanity lurking beneath my pious hospitality? Was it to teach me to hold my plans loosely? (How soon I have forgotten the lockdown's lessons!) Was it to give our two families needed time alone? Or was the cause of the cancellation rooted in the essential brokenness of things? The unexpected family time a way God redeemed the apparent loss?

I do not know. But I believe that despite the evil and chaos expanding in all directions everywhere, God redeems. Merciful, God takes smashed bits and the miry stuff of life and makes something lovely—we await this.

*

When everything stops, we are gifted a glimpse of something profound. One Friday night during the COVID lockdown, my husband and I were picking up carryout in a neighborhood where (pre-pandemic) you could dance all night at the Vogue or get a tattoo or indulge in a pineapple basil popsicle. Ours was the only car parked on the street. The quiet felt apocalyptic. Like the last trump was about to sound, that last obliterating light stunning the world's eyes.

Such a strange pause, this, when the world stumbled to a near stop. I wonder: if our communities kept Sabbaths, would the pause not have felt quite so strange? Maybe we would've felt, in some weird sense, like we were in the year of Jubilee.

*

Excitement over cancellations and even my philosophizing skim over the brick and bone reality of the pandemic: those who did not have compensation to cover their forced leave, the bleeding of businesses, the stock market slapping its nadir, the elderly and ill who had to weigh the pros and cons of exposing themselves to a potentially life-threatening illness to buy prescriptions and eggs (if there were even any to be found). Cancellations often root in obstacles ranging from the unpleasant to the deadly: traffic, an emergency meeting at work, sudden illness, tornados, blizzards, accidents.

In 2020 when the world was canceled, a member of our former church in Addis Ababa was on his way to the airport. At age thirty, Caleb was the youngest elder in the church. He had recently moved from London, origin of his late father (who died in a plane crash in Kenya when Caleb was a child), to Ethiopia where his mother called home. He had a vision for community development and opened a café across the street from our church. One Sunday during a visit to Ethiopia, my husband and I enjoyed lunch at Caleb's Bake and Brew, walked upstairs to a windowed space for gathering. The wall facing the descending stairs was full of photographs of the beautiful people on Caleb's heart.

Caleb never made it to the airport.

How to grapple with this gravest of cancellations: the annulment of life?

Baked bread and planted gardens and snow days dissolve to frippery before death. I feel ashamed of my giddiness for the end of school, like a kid caught laughing at a funeral. How could I have celebrated movie-watching and book-reading when fellow humans were suffering and dying, dead?

How cold it is here at the brink of the void.

I wonder what could be learned in the isolation of our cells: kitchen, living room, bedroom. Cancellations invite us not to binge-watching—but to pondering life's essential questions. When much that occupies our time and forms the stuff of personal meaning evaporates, we are forced to face what is left. In the emptiness (or *la vide*, as the French existentialists would call it), we have a choice to continue distracting ourselves or to engage with what scares us: those questions of purpose and identity, the whys. Even if we will never find a satisfactory answer here on this time-bound planet.

In the cessations, the failings, the fallow seasons, I am reminded to unclench my plans, my life, everything I have. Because truly there is nothing I have.

In these days that feel like the hem of the world, it is profoundly humbling to realize how uncertain life is, how feeble I fall before the future's face.[28]

I'll buy bread today, God willing.

Talk to you soon, God willing.

We will make it okay, all shall be well, yes, all shall be well,
God willing,

God wills,

God will.[29]

kitchen tabernacles:

on hunger

Food is God's love made delectable.

—*Norman Wirzba*, Food and Faith: A Theology of Eating

B reakfast, like all meals, is a grace. After an evening and night of emptiness, the morning offers an opportunity for replenishment. As a student in France, I would break my fast with little cups of strong coffee, baguettes that crinkled when you cut them, real jam, and butter I could eat with a spoon. With my in-laws in Ethiopia, I break my fast with torn bits of spiced fried bread in bowls or eggs bright with jalapeño or injera heavy with the impression of lamb. Here in Indianapolis, I break my fast with oats of all varieties. Of course, there is always tea or coffee. Somehow, when the belly has been scraped clean like the new morning, breakfast tastes like no other meal of the day.

Though breakfast is my favorite, I love all meals. I love how each earth rotation structures itself around plated grace: breakfast, lunch, and dinner. At each meal, we are invited to pause, to hush the bustle of our hours. Wearied, we are invited to sit and rest.

And enjoy.

I enjoy sweet potatoes roasted in olive oil and salt, the burn of new naan, the way kale bites. I enjoy how spaghetti squash shouts yellow on a white plate, how fizzy water giggles in a glass. My favorite part of a meal is dessert. I eat dark chocolate almost every day (a health food full of antioxidants, I am told), and let triangles bleed over my tongue in the colors of coffee and berry and oak. How my heart leaps when, at the end of an excellent meal, the host announces the name of a fabulous sweetmeat to come.

The whole process of nourishing delights. Cooking expresses a divinely seeded creativity, throwing dashes of this and that like paint spatter. Recipes like sheet music, cups and teaspoons the musical notation. Eating, I enjoy the way my hungering stomach begins to fill, how energy awakens in my veins. It feels satisfying to devour the creative work of my own hands, the fruit of labor and time.

Or, to give thanks for the fruit of another's labor. (Beyond count, the meals others have served me.) Even if it was my own hands that whisked and minced, I am still indebted to the lives snuffed to sustain mine. I have ended another being's circulation, whether of blood or chlorophyll, to revive my own. Even the means to purchase the life-bled fare (oranges snapped from the bough, finless salmon) is a gift of God. Each year hundreds of millions of human beings hunger, while I am blessed to excess.[1]

Thrice daily, I am called to thanksgiving.

There is something divine in the tripartite ingestion of daily bread—something holy in the routine act of eating itself. I am reminded of St. Paul's words: *Whether you eat or drink, do all to the glory of God.*[2] And poet Kahlil Gibran's: "But since you must kill to eat, and rob the newly born of its mother's milk to quench your thirst, let it be an act of worship."[3]

David agrees: *O taste and see that the LORD is good!*[4] Professor Norman Wirzba writes that the Latin term for discernment and understanding, *sapientia*, is linked to *sapere*, meaning "to taste." Tasting offers an immediacy of contact that gives intimate knowledge.[5] In the way steamed broccoli gleams emerald, in the puffed heat of jasmine rice, in the flavors of wine and walnut—I taste, I know the goodness of God. Through the intimacy of taste on tongue, I understand more shades of divine sweetness. Strawberries in hand-whipped cream declare God's glory, and sautéed onions sing a chorus of praise.

Perhaps Simone Weil, whose obsession with food infuses her writing, was envisioning rich red bowls of *bœuf bourguignon* or oaky glasses of Merlot when she wrote, "The beauty of the world is Christ's tender smile for us coming through matter."[6] Weil seems to say that with each sip and spoonful, we are invited to revel in beauty (the incarnation of God's mercy and grace, God's God-ness), even as God's presence within us is awakened. Meal-taking then can be a kind of sacrament, a prayer.

But how do laden tables transfigure into altars, ladder-back chairs into pews? What leads us to this space of gratitude, leaves of lettuce splayed like hymn books?

Hunger.

Each day structures itself around meals (those tabernacles endlessly vanishing and reappearing) not because of human strength—but human weakness. Weakness presses me to pause my labors, opening a door to divine hospitality: God giving Godself in the form of bread and wine, apple and milk. Need carves out a space in my stomach ready to be filled with the savory and the sweet. Hunger, my perpetual inability to self-sustain, invites me to enjoy God's table of good things.

"Isn't it gracious of God," my mom would say, "that we have the sense of taste?" God could have created humans without taste buds. God could have created just one earthly crop. God could have created humans to survive on straight mush or even made us purely spiritual entities that don't sup or sip at all. Taste, and the sheer kaleidoscope of foods that exist for human pleasure, shout God's extravagant graciousness. Grace: walking through the local international market and gawking at dragon fruit and jackfruit and mamey sapote and soursop.

In *The Supper of the Lamb*, chef Robert Farrar Capon writes, "Food is the daily sacrament of unnecessary goodness, ordained for a continual remembrance that the world will always be more delicious than it is useful."[7] Furry kiwi, the onion's flamelike curvature, ground cherries suspended in their little paper lanterns all remind me that God is not a practical utilitarian, but a great lover of delight. All that humans savor on their tongues exists out of divine desire and is divinely upheld out of love.[8]

*

That humans were created to perpetually need, and perpetually enjoy, delights but puzzles me. It is a great mystery that life depends on violent death: the severing and burning of animal flesh, the skinning and boiling of sentient fruit and vegetable. My kitchen is full of instruments of violence: pounders, mincers, graters, blenders, knives. Perhaps reflecting on his own farm, Wendell Berry writes, "To live, we must daily break the body and shed the blood of Creation."[9]

Even more incomprehensible is the reality of millions of human beings who cannot find food or buy food—and die each year.[10] Walking along cobblestone streets in Ethiopia, I pass skinny boys squatting together, scooping out leftovers thrown out in a plastic bag. I pass bony mothers draped in languid babies who press the tips of their five gathered fingers to their mouths in the universal sign of hunger. Hunger can be a grace but also a groan, an expression of the world's inherent brokenness. Though primarily a source of delight in my middle-class American life, hunger is a source of continual strain for much of the world.

On a personal level, the reality of my perpetual need means I can't go more than a few hours without feeling hungry. I can't eat a week's worth of food and then buckle myself to my desk chair for a week of uninterrupted labor. I must eat and drink little by little, day by day, as the Israelites gathered manna in the wilderness.[11] The miraculous, honeyed wafers only lasted one day. Manna flickered over the sand then flew. Excess decayed to maggots. Each day, I must gather grace like manna, because each day my needing growls.

For me at present, grace-gathering (or rather, grace-receiving) looks like nestling within my wicker porch chair before my husband wakes up, Scripture, journal, and tea in hand. It looks like ingesting divine words like honey, letting the syllables melt over my tongue, or gulping them like sweet water in a wilderness. It looks like listening beyond birdsong and jackhammers to the Spirit's voice. It looks like unburdening my heart onto my Father's. It looks like silence.

It looks like Christ—eating of Christ at each moment of every day.

Weil—who at age five refused sugar in solidarity with soldiers on the frontlines of World War II, who at age thirty-four died of cardiac failure partly from self-starvation, who knew the shape of hunger—writes that we cannot store "the energy that comes on high" any more than the Israelites could store manna. Our energy-gathering should not just be a daily act, but a moment-by-moment one. Speaking of Christ, Weil writes, "We can only ask to have him now."[12]

My weekly two hours at church or those few moments on the porch are not enough to sustain my soul. They will never be enough. They are only crumbs compared to the whole life of dependence I am called to, a daily breathing in and breathing out prayer. Eating grace like oxygen. Practicing the presence of God with Brother Lawrence.[13] Playing missionary Frank Laubach's "Game with Minutes."[14] Praying without ceasing like St. Paul.[15] I am called to redeem each moment in time, consecrating it for worship. Building tabernacles of breakfast tables and turning spoons into instruments of praise.

In pouring water, I need you.
In pouring myself, I need you.
Pour yourself into me.

I imagine myself walking through each step and stumbling of the day: boiling water and scraping plates, the commutes and conversations. I imagine each time I breathe, the LORD is holding me still, and the LORD's mouth is over my mouth. The LORD is breathing each full breath of my lungs. Each breath is given. Every emptying of carbon dioxide opens me to the grace of holy oxygen. I was born on life support, a kind of divine CPR.

My soul burns through grace like my metabolism does food. As soon as one meal ends, I think towards the next, and I rarely feel full for long. My husband laughs at how much and how often I eat. "You're hungry already?" he will ask, with degrees of incredulity that diminish as our years of marriage increase. Recently, I've found this frustrating. I just want to feel full, once and for all.

Here is what I struggle with: how could the unending, omnipotent bread of grace be so fragile and fleeting? For Weil, the supernatural bread (like manna) is as ephemeral as dew. It vaporizes the moment our attention shifts—the moment we break out of prayer, out of practicing God's presence. Though infinitely potent, divine energy evaporates the moment we cease to desire it.[16]

Why won't divine bread sate my soul for more than mere moments?

Perhaps the very limits of God's grace (the manna-like portions) are a grace in themselves. Perhaps God gives Godself like bread crumbs in a dark forest to lead us, bit by bit, to open spaces. Perhaps we can only survive God's kisses, because the full consummation of union would burn us into oblivion. Perhaps God only gives us little bites of the divine, moment by moment, because if God gave Godself fully, we would perish, stomachs, minds, and souls exploded and split, consumed.

*

Not feeling hungry, not knowing my continual need of divine grace, gets dangerous. When I was living at home, my family would spend summer vacations with my aunt and uncle in Fort Lauderdale. My Uncle Tom was a retired businessman, a millionaire who furnished a penthouse by the ocean like a mini Louvre: gold filigree and a gold sink and a whole chandelier of Swarovski crystal. He was one of the most generous and wise souls I have ever known and relished lavishing us with gifts like it was Christmas in July. A single-income family of seven (for whom going out to eat was mostly grabbing two things from McDonald's Dollar Menu), we felt we had stumbled into some kind of heaven, the little castle hovering above the building blocks and toy cars of the city.

And we gorged. Uncle Tom would drive us in his latest Mercedes to the fanciest restaurants in town (those dim, plush places). I ate Mahi Mahi and macaroni and cheese with truffles and sea bass and shrimp and scallops and filet mignon and scalloped potatoes and lobster bisque and seared Ahi tuna with bottles of Perrier. Most of my family would be too full after dinner to tackle dessert, but not me. I gulped cannolis and chocolate mousse and key lime pie and lava cakes and slabs of what Uncle Tom called the best carrot cake ever. I would eat so much, I would sometimes crumple onto a satiny couch, nauseous and moaning. I would eat so much, I would play a game of pacing myself to be able to stomach the next meal. I would eat so much, I would forget what hunger felt like, and, oddly enough, begin to miss wanting and appreciating food.

Gluttony, rather than sating my hunger, opened up a bigger, deeper one.

Overeating can still be a struggle for me. Gluttony offers not enough but more: more cake and more Camembert and more warm rolls pillowed in folds of cloth. I want so much to be satisfied once and for all and believe that stuffing my stomach will achieve this. As if more will satisfy. As if something wonderful exists beyond enough-ness. As if eating the whole monstrous slab of champagne raspberry cake from the bakery will give me the wholeness I am seeking. Perhaps it does, for the few moments I float in a sugar daze.

But then I feel sick and cannot sleep with the "food baby" (as my friend calls it) rolling over the waist of my jeans. Though in American culture gluttony feels like a minor sin I can make up for later with an extra-long run and a quick "sorry" flung to the skies, it is still sin (one of the seven deadly ones). And sin induces guilt; it alienates me from God. I resolve to eat no dessert for a whole five days at least (chocolate not included).

Humans can only enjoy so much. (I remember my Papa saying before one holiday meal, the satin-cloaked folding tables burdened under dishes flooded in butter, "I wish I had two stomachs to devote to this meal.") When I overeat, eating ceases to become enjoyable. No matter how much I try to increase or prolong my enjoyment of food with increased quantities, I only end up with heartburn. Excess manna rots.

But appetites move beyond just food. King David knew the dangers of being trapped by appetites. After amassing wives and castles and kingdoms and daughters and sons and war trophies and anecdotes of holy behavior, after napping while his armies fought his wars, after the boredom of satiation—he lingered on the roof, leered at Bathsheba's naked body, and tumbled into adultery, murder, and the death of his infant son.[17]

There is a reason we, who purchase movies and music, jujitsu and jingles, are called consumers. Even lovers talk of their longing with the language of consumption. Humans consume. Weil writes that money, ambition, celebrity, power, our loved ones—anything that fuels our actions—is like bread. And losing such soul-deep attachments is like dying of hunger.[18] Food (or anything) consumed in gluttony only famishes the soul, stokes the appetite for more, and never sates.

Looking beyond ourselves, we can see how gluttony of any kind also poisons our relationships with others, and God. Wirzba argues that food is not primarily about consumption but self-offering: the offering of God's body to be eaten in human mouths in the Eucharist and on our daily plates, the offering of our own bodies and resources to feed others, both physically and spiritually. But "if we give our hearts to all that we consume in this world, this world becomes not the food that nourishes but the food that fuels fear and vanities that prevent us from offering our lives to each other and to God."[19]

Gluttony blocks our love.

Yet humans continue to pursue what never fulfills. Weil explains, "This unsatisfied appetite, the desire to keep on increasing, is due precisely to a desire for contact with universal beauty."[20] Beautiful plates of nourishment only veil God if I worship them as gods. My physical hunger is merely symptomatic of a spiritual one. The gaping in my belly is really the gaping of my soul that philosopher Blaise Pascal wrote of.[21] What I seek in Buddha bowls and kombucha and flourless chocolate cake is beyond physical energy and aesthetic pleasure: the real, the living God.

*

In hunger, food satisfies more deeply. Meals after a day gardening or hiking transcend the usual routine of eating. One of the meals I enjoyed most was when my youngest sister Olivia was born. Still in the hospital a couple of days after her birth, she was being tested for a serious complication. A memory: my dad hanging up the hospital phone after a conversation with a friend who had called to check in. Repeating the friend's words, he said, "Joy comes in the morning."[22] I remember the tears in both of my parents' eyes. A senior in high school, I had never fasted more than lunch before, but felt that this, when my baby sister's life was flickering, would be no better time to begin.

That day, it felt odd but right to forego the morning oats. There was something freeing, even empowering in my refusal to satiate my physical hunger. *Man shall not live by bread alone, but by every word that proceeds from the mouth of God,*[23] I said to my gut, imagining myself (perhaps rather dramatically) in a desert with the Tempter. In class, I wearied under my small hunger, under the burden I carried called Olivia.

But it seemed that God crept close, that my emptiness cradled me within an intimate, invisible aura, kept me in some kind of grace. When my stomach groaned, I would remember the words of my fasting warrior mother: "Whenever you feel the hunger pains, pray."

That evening, my dad took my siblings and me out to a local cafeteria. After a day without food, it seemed like the best meal I had ever tasted: creamy macaroni and cheese crusted with cheddar, sweet butter with bits of soft clover rolls, perhaps some savory green beans or mashed potatoes with gravy or flaking tilapia with tartar sauce and cocktail sauce both. Olivia, we learned, had tested negative for the complication. She could come home with us soon. Oh, that meal was sweet.

The tradition of fasting roots throughout the Bible: in times of prayer, mourning, anguish, preparation, punishment, discernment, repentance, compassion. Leaders in the early church viewed fasting as a spiritual practice that deepened one's walk with God. Wirzba adds that fasting can be an act of solidarity with those who hunger, one that reminds us how food is a gracious gift not to be taken for granted, how it does not exist merely for our own pleasure—but to be offered and received in community.[24]

In this way, fasting can be an act of redemption.

In my own life, I've seen how fasting redeems, jarring my slumbering soul awake. Consistently filled and content with more than enough food, I can march through the day's routines self-satisfied with my illusory self-sufficiency. It is easy to forget that without God I can do nothing.[25]

But hunger pangs, like any pain, course through me like an electric shock. My eyes are opened: to the color of rose clouds at dawn, to the shapes of strangers' faces, to the reality of my constant need, to the presence of God enfolded in towels and pots and grocery store carts. Fasting forms a sort of tangible line tying my heart to God's. In the echoes of an empty stomach, how near the Universe Maker feels!

However beautiful its moments of clarity, fasting has mostly been a struggle for me. During the COVID lockdown, that season of global mourning, my husband and I decided to fast until three p.m. (the hour the Lamb died on the cross). Only seven hours to go, I thought as the day began. I tried not to look at the clock as I tapped away at my keyboard, in the same way my students try not to look at the clock when they can't wait for the bell to ring and free them from this French grammar nonsense. Only four hours. Now only two!

With an effort, I would shove my glance heavenward again. But I kept self-sabotaging my attempt at spiritual practice, missing the truth: fasting is not to cultivate a greater awareness of my stomach, but a greater awareness of God. Emptiness that does not seek a Godward filling is meaningless. As Merton says, "Recollection without faith confines the spirit in a prison without light or air."[26]

Hunger for its own sake falls flat.

Hunger is sanctified by the object of its attention. For Weil, it is attention (prayer, practicing God's presence) that saves us, as the diseased, wilderness-wandering Israelites found salvation in attending to the bronze serpent.[27] And it is misplaced attention, an attention on the surface of an earthly gift rather than on the divinity that animates it, that causes our demise. Eve provoked the downfall of humanity because she ate what she should have only looked at.

What does it mean to look and not eat?

Perhaps fasting holds a key. In abstaining at mealtimes, we look at plates of food being devoured around us and fill the emptiness in our stomachs with prayers. St. Basil the Great preached that fasting reverses Adam's desire and greed in eating the forbidden fruit.[28] In cultivating the practice of looking and not eating, we redeem ancient greed and transform it into prayer.

Perhaps looking and not eating could also mean eating physically without seeking to be ultimately sated in food. I can rejoice in the gift of pho by seeing it as a window to the Giver. Merton again: "For when our intention is directed to God, our very use of material things sanctifies both them and us, provided we use them without selfishness and without presumption, glad to receive them from Him Who loves us and Whose love is all we desire."[29] When gazing skyward, the one who eats the pho and the pho itself illumine the One who set the table in the first place.

What if the object of my hunger—physical, mental, emotional, spiritual—was God? God the Unconsumable, the Fire Who Consumes. David said those who seek the LORD lack no good thing.[30] St. Matthew said those who hunger and thirst for righteousness will be satisfied.[31] Jesus called himself the Bread of Life—the ultimate Manna—and the source of living water.[32] Mary said that though God sent the rich away empty, he has filled the hungry with good things.[33] Her empty womb bloomed with the Redeemer of All Things. Her hunger was a grace.

And how she was filled!

Only beyond the sky will I no longer need to be hungry to be filled. Only beyond the sky will I be fully sated, not in consumption, but in perfect attention to God, an attention more satisfying than any earthly bread or wine. Only beyond the sky will this staring be the same as supping.[34] Only beyond the sky will my soul expand enough to bear the burden of glory beyond all comparison.[35]

Though on earth I tasted God on my tongue in honey wine and cake, caught God in glimpses of a grapefruit's sunset skin and a pomegranate's jeweled symmetry, beyond the sky I will meet God in unfathomable intimacy.

I will see God face to face.[36]

Utterly attentive to the Lover of my soul, I will be able to hold all the God-ness of God: to consume all and not be consumed.

the garden queue:

on waiting

I will be waiting here,
for your silence to break,
for your soul to shake,
for your love to wake.

—Rumi

"That wasn't so bad," I said. My family and I had just purchased tickets at a small tourist office a few minutes' walk from the marble-laden castle of Versailles. The queue had been quick; we were speeding ahead of those other tourists buying tickets at the chateau itself. Decked in blaring white sneakers and fanny packs, they were easily spotted. After a brief bag inspection at the crenelated gates, we stopped for a second. First, to gape at the fortress of a house gleaming golden under an unimpeded July sun. Then, at the sprawled, looping lines of tourists spread across the massive cobblestone road funneling to a tiny doorway. Rick Steves had warned Versailles would be busy, but I was not prepared for the wait ahead.

Four hours. We ate our lunch standing, talked and talked standing, burned slowly in the heat standing. Finally, we pushed our way through into high rooms padded in red silk and weighted with layers of crown molding, ceilings burdened with gods ascending into clouds.

In the end, we preferred Versailles's park-wide gardens: open to real sky, spaces expansive enough to be alone in, even in the height of tourist season. To enter these gardens, there was hardly a wait at all.

*

Much of life is lived in lines. Lines pushing grocery carts in the rush-hour glut after work. Lines at the post office holding a heavy cardboard box. Lines for the best Pad Thai in town on a Friday night. Lines to speak to a real person after shouting at a robot. Lines to see muscled arms toss a ball. Lines to cram against other shoulders to hear strums and beats. Lines of sweaty, dripping bodies waiting to slip down a water slide in seconds. Lines for everything humans deem desirable. I don't like lines, but I'm trying to see the gifts therein, trying to believe gifts are there to be found.

*

Here is a challenge to myself: don't waste the line. The busy part of me, the taskmaster obsessed with efficiency, tells me waiting can be put to good use: email correspondence, mental meal planning, marking my way through stacks of my students' quizzes. During grad school, I wrote essay drafts sitting in planes and airports. One of the modern Bible paraphrases was transcribed on subway commutes.

If the line is long enough and slow enough, especially if there is seating, like at the doctor's or license branch, I sometimes read. Ever since I was a little girl, I've made a habit of bringing a book almost everywhere. Suddenly, the mauve walls and staid paintings dissolve, and I enter a sphere of infinitely more interest: through the wardrobe to biting firs and the frosty lamppost, jumping over bends in time, pressing axle grease over my lips on the Oregon Trail.

At Versailles, we redeemed the hours in conversation, in enjoying each other's presence as much as we could. At least we were waiting together, and together we would share a memory of the longest line we had ever known.

*

Despite my best efforts, somehow I find it easy to languish in lines. Somehow, it feels right to be miserable and bored. It's easy to ignore the efficient taskmaster and scroll through the endless, mostly meaningless minutiae on my phone. It's easy to pour out my precious few earthly minutes in staring and wishing I was not here.

But maybe the staring is not wasted. Maybe it's okay to ignore the taskmaster. Maybe the line invites me into a moment of space and quietude. Here is a forced pause in the whirl of to-do lists I am knotted and bound in, tripped and whipped by.

Here, I stop.

My heart rate slows.

At the dentist's office, my phone is poised for action, my thumbs at attention. All day I've been swatting at tasks like fired tennis balls. It seems my mind's been executing six different duties each minute: photocopying quizzes, coordinating remedial work for lagging students, penciling lesson plans, scheduling a last-minute parent-teacher conference, and on the list unravels. Then, the sudden pause in the waiting room like brakes jammed to the floorboards of a speeding car. (Funny how we rush to make appointments on time, only to wait.)

I know I can check my email (again) in an attempt to feel productive. But somehow I feel there is meaning waiting, meaning pulsing beneath the surface of this moment, if I will just be still. I stuff my phone into my purse at my feet and try to practice presence. I notice: whiffs of metallic prongs and rubber gloves, the scandal muttering through the TV, the way an elderly man has looped his wife's handbag over his knee, the empty chair next to him holding a book on hummingbirds.

But observation for observation's sake falls flat. Emptiness for its own sake empties. Solitude needs a center. Without faith, I'll find myself in the lightless, airless prison Merton describes.[1] In the dentist's office, I try to hear what is underneath all that I sense. I try to hear the Spirit.

Then: whispers.

Painful, this process of unlearning efficiency. It allows not only spaces and gaps, but Godward ones. Instead of checking my text messages as I wait at the dinner table for my husband to wash his hands, I am learning to permit a few seconds of unplanned silence to listen, to be aware. Instead of occupying my mind with battalions of distraction, I am learning to be curious about what God will say in the silence. Instead of planning the weekend out in Monday morning traffic, I am learning prayer. Spaces of waiting can open into little cells of contemplation, solitude, silence.

*

As much as a door to the interior, perhaps the queue also opens outward, extending an invitation to communal presence.

I am in line at Walmart after a long day of teaching (But what day of teaching is not long?). Mechanical blips mark the seconds. I notice. I notice the candy-colored stacks of gum. I notice the magazine headlines with yet another revolutionary way to lose ten pounds. I notice the cashier's nametag. Her name is French. As a French teacher living in the middle of Indiana, even the remotest connection to the language excites me. "*Parlez-vous français?*" I ask.

The woman looks up, and in her eyes it's as if a curtain is thrust back. "*Oui, je parle français!*" She tells me she is from Haiti. She tells me of the hurricanes. She expands, multidimensional, from the flat, blue Walmart vest into a human being shaped by story. And perhaps I become to her more than another flat face in a ceaseless battery of consuming faces. These few seconds on earth we share, suddenly, strangely.

*

But what about the long-term waiting, that gut-crushing, crossbeam-splinters-in-your-back kind? Lines at Walmart are a spoonful of cream compared to the labor of waiting for an acceptance letter, a callback, a kidney transplant, a homecoming, or, in my case, the conception of a child. My husband and I have been trying for nearly a year, and each passing month falls like a stone on the heart.

The Sunday-morning faithful say God's timing is best. However cliché it sounds, in my own life this has proven true, even if I have had to adjust my meaning of "best," entrust its definition to God. God calls me to remember the ebenezers, those tangible reminders in stone and ash telling stories of divine goodness. Reading the Old Testament, I've noticed that when God speaks to the Israelites, he often begins by stating what he has done for them in the past: *I am the LORD your God who brought you out of the land of Egypt.*[2] It's when the Israelites forget this that they stray.

A closed door can be a grace. Like all the boys I had crushes on who never noticed me—until my husband. Like the house we knew was the one—but wasn't, because another was better.

Or like when I was just about to graduate from university and didn't have a job yet. I had applied for a position in a French government program teaching English to French students. I knew it was meant for me. But a formulaic email stated I'd been waitlisted, and ultimately, I was not chosen.

Plan B: find a job. I sent out letters to all of the publishing houses I could find in my hometown. I brandished a straight-A transcript, a double major in English and French, a stack of awards, completed internships with respected local organizations. No one replied.

And then weeks before graduation, one of my professors emailed me an opportunity to teach French at an international school in Ethiopia. "Just pray about it," she wrote. I did. In a baffling flash of six weeks, I accepted the position, raised enough funds to go (or rather, God miraculously provided despite my reluctant efforts), and found myself on a plane to Addis Ababa.

I entered Ethiopia, emptied of the world I knew, and left four years later, gift-laden: the hundred-fold family Jesus promises, lifelong friends, my husband. We have nailed an Ethiopian cross in our dining room. It is silver.

I wonder what the distinction is between active waiting on God's timing and passive complacency. What if waiting on God's timing means carrying out the timing, like a midwife? And how do I know what God's timing even is? I may never know the answers to these questions, but I do know that the entrance to Ethiopia was something I could not have sought on my own. It could only have arrived as a simple, unexpected grace. What I truly wanted, or perhaps needed (Is there a difference between the two?), was something that had not even entered my consciousness.

It wasn't Versailles's opulent corridors that satisfied, but the gardens.

*

The waiting for that divine timing can be excruciating. The dark distance between the request and the request granted gapes painful—but sometimes exhilarating, too. At a speakeasy lit with fairy lights, my friend and I sip cocktails. In her fishnet tights and sparkly black shoes, she gushes over her beau. She cannot wait to be married. "If he would bend on one knee right here, right now," she said. "I would say yes." Even as she mouths her longing into words, her face lights up against the dim.

My husband and I have been married for almost five years, and while I would trade nothing for the anchoring depth of our love now, while I would never want to return to the tantalizing, unsteady jitters of courtship, I sometimes recall that premarital pursuit with a kind of wistfulness. The unknown was dangerous and exciting in a way, starlit as it was. We had not seen each other's bodies. We had not shared a bed, or a kitchen. We had not yet toed the aisle in tux and dress. So much lay ahead to look forward to. As yet unformed by reality, those folded fairylands took on fantastical colors. What was not yet could be anything, could be as wide as my imagination and my dreams.

And there was something sweet about the yearning. I remember those terrible moments after dates in cheap cafés, saying goodbye to my fiancé at that street in his neighborhood in the dark. I remember kissing him, and the longing to take him home with me was a palpable thing, a heavy presence in my gut, something not yet born but itching to be. Even in that keen craving, the craving itself, the pure absinthe of desire, showed me I was alive and that I loved and that good things lay ahead.

This season of waiting for a child unsettles. As each cycle begins, a fresh hope begins. And as each cycle ends, that hope dies. But in this season of yearning together, waiting together, we root together. That there is something ahead that we desire enlivens our spirits, even as at times that same desire seems to enfeeble them. Expectation, hopeful expectation, is a gift.

"This time is precious," I say to my friend, her form shadowed bright against the winter dark. "Enjoy the mystery and excitement of this season. You'll never get it back."

Even as I say these words, I know they are meant for me, too.

*

My grandparents have already had—and sometimes lost—the loves they fell for, the babies they prayed for, the careers they sweated for, the grandbabies (and great-grandbabies) they hinted for. My Grandpa lives in a makeshift bedroom walled in hastily sewn curtains. He awakes alone in bed, shuffles to the bathroom on his walker, balances food to his mouth at the kitchen table. These few cells compose his whole world.

"It's heck gettin' old," our 80-something-year-old neighbor would say before he died in a morphine haze on a cot in a dark bedroom. Joe was a farmer who would force himself up on his John Deere or on his walker to water the roses. He knew if he stopped, he would stop forever. He had to tend something to stay alive. He had to have something to wait for.

Waiting is part of what keeps us alive.

*

There is a sense that the longer the wait is, the more valuable the object of waiting. At a famous local bakery, I feel I've stepped into a rococo painting or Marie Antoinette's boudoir. Pearls string around wispy chandeliers, servers flit in white ruffled aprons, garlands of artificial flowers brush ivory crown-molding, tri-layered cakes tower frostily in polished glass domes. To pass the time, my husband and I stare at framed photos of celebrities with cakes. We've ordered two slices (champagne raspberry for me, German chocolate for him), and the wait lengthens. "It shouldn't take this long to cut two slices of cake," my husband says. I agree.

But then I wonder: maybe it's all part of the game. Fast-food restaurants pride themselves in brown-bagging warmed-up meat patties in seconds—but neither the servers nor the consumers have any illusions they are transacting anything of value. Maybe the extra-long wait for the extra-long slice is intentional: waiting builds anticipation, heightens mouth watering, fills the expectant cake-eater with visions of a confectionary heaven. It shows the worth of the thing sought—even if, in the end, the object does not satisfy.

*

I know I will always be waiting on something. When I graduated, I wanted a job. When I had a job, I wanted to be married. After getting married, I now want children. And the rest of my story is not yet written. I may never hold a child of my own body. But I do see a pattern in my own vaporous life: once one prayer is answered, another will be birthed in its place. My husband and I will always be waiting: for a package in the mail, a visa, a job, a healing, a reconciliation, a next step. I know I will never be satisfied here.

And maybe that's the point.

We dream of gilded castles when all along our deepest desire is to return to the Garden.

Or rather, the One who breathed the Garden into being. In his famous poem "Dark Night of the Soul," St. John of the Cross burns for his Beloved.

> On a dark night,
> fired with love's urgent longings
> — ah, the sheer grace! —
> I went out unseen,
> my house being now all stilled.

It is dark, the narrator is alone, hidden, hungering. He has no guide but his desire, no guide but the dark. And the desire—the longing itself—is a grace.

> O guiding night!
> O night more lovely than the dawn!
> O night that has united
> the Lover with his beloved,
> transforming the beloved in her Lover.[3]

Night as guide. Dark as a space of union. Lightlessness as transformative, as a sharpening and shaping unto holiness. I pray to burn, to be enlivened by, this kind of desire, one that snuffs all others. That I would see the object of my waiting in every queue and jam, the object of my waiting being divine. Perhaps my impatience roots in misprioritized longing. Though we wait a lifetime for the divine consummation, to seek God now requires no queue at all.

Part Three:
Conception

veiled faces:

on
unknowing

When thou seest . . . thy faculties bereft of their capacity for any interior exercise, be not afflicted by this, but rather consider it a great happiness, since God is freeing thee from thyself and taking the matter from thy hands.

—*St. John of the Cross*, Dark Night of the Soul

A child hides in the dark of my womb. His eyes are shut, his ears holding only muffles in their hollows. He is at rest in darkness and silence, like a buried seed or a worm bound in chrysalis.

My eyes are shut, my ears inept. I cannot see the being swaddled within my skin, though I feel his heel against my palm. Though I long to see his face. For nine months we must wait—until the painful revelation.

*

In this season of pregnancy, I know so little by the organs I've relied on most: eye and ear. Now knowing has become attention to feeling: a widening within my being, stretched skin, a new gravity, nameless flutters.

If I know so little of a presence so near my body, within my own body, how much less do I know of everything else: bird music and the way of abiding oaks, stardust and the delicate complexity of cells.

If the fear of the LORD is the beginning of wisdom, perhaps fear, this sense of awe and wonder before the unknown, is a step towards knowing anything at all.[1]

*

"I am learning to listen to the Spirit," my friend says as we walk, gathering breathfuls of weighty August air. She is telling me how she felt divine flutterings, followed the whispers despite fear and trembling, and stumbled upon the unexpected grace of a new friendship.

"How did you know it was God speaking to you?" I always ask this question of my Spirit-sensitive friends. I struggle to know myself.

"I don't know," she says. And her explanation muddies in my mind. But in my memory she seems to be holding her gut, where her womb would be.

*

The prophet Isaiah has been my manna of late, manna meaning in Hebrew, "What is it?"

I do not have an answer.

Isaiah says again and again: *see, hear.* See the awful reality of the God-Who-Is electrifying the universe. Hear the divine voice in wave-roar and whisper. *Hear, you deaf, and look, you blind, that you may see!*[2]

Judgment darkens around the blind and deaf; deafness and blindness descend with the darkness.

*

The word "mystery" stems from the Greek *mystērion* meaning, "secret rite or doctrine, consisting of purifications, sacrificial offerings, processions, songs." *Mystērion* stems from *mystēs*, "one who has been initiated," which in turn stems from *myein*, "to close, shut"; "perhaps referring to the lips (in secrecy) or to the eyes (only initiates were allowed to see the sacred rites)."[3] Or perhaps, to the ears.

In C.S. Lewis's *Till We Have Faces*, the beautiful, innocent princess Psyche is chosen to be sacrificed as the Great Offering to purify the drought-stricken land of Glome and sate the faceless goddess Ungit, the womb and mother of all. Priests and temple girls and townsfolk accompany a makeup-masked Psyche to the Holy Tree, where she is bound and left alone to be devoured by Ungit's son, the Shadowbrute. Psyche's sister Orual describes Ungit's music as "all holy, deadly—dark, detestable, maddening noises."[4] The darkness of the holy grates on the ears.

In the morning, Psyche is gone.

After searching for her beloved sister, Orual finally finds her in a flourishing valley. Psyche recounts how the West-wind (whom the people misperceived as the Shadowbrute) liberated her, gathered her in his arms, and flew his new bride to a glorious home of pillared courts and tables set with fruit and wine. A beatific Psyche describes the splendor of her immortal husband, but confesses that she has never seen him. "He comes to me only in the holy darkness. He says I mustn't—not yet—see his face or know his name."[5]

"What kind of a lover must this be who forbids his bride to see his face?" asks Orual later.[6]

What kind of God hides himself?

The veil between dark-hid realities and the brick and bone world closes like eyelids—a weighty blanket that muffles holy songs and hides angel brushwork. I am called to rest in a God I can see only by his traces and effects. To trust not in horses and chariots I can hold—bank accounts and muscular cars and familiar hands—but in a God I cannot.[7]

To walk, led by flutters. The pregnancy books, those mysterious guides seeking to initiate women into the rites of motherhood, say it can be difficult for a first-time mother to discern the movement of her unborn. To feel the difference between bubbles of gas and a quickening child. Empty echoes and fullness itself. Mothers tell me the discernment becomes easier with time.

Until then, I walk continually blinded and blind. I await the veil torn like a womb in birthing.

*

Yet I hunger to know. My ears strain for divine vibrations. Why do I still feel blind and stumbling, tensile fingers spread as if in uncertain worship?

Orual wrestles with the mysterious opacity of the gods: how they hide behind veils and speak in riddles. She longs for a world where "the gods show themselves clearly and don't torment men with glimpses, nor unveil to one what they hide from another, nor ask you to believe what contradicts your eyes and ears and nose and tongue and fingers."[8] If I'm honest, I often long for this kind of world, too.

My hands grip truth: *And I will lead the blind in a way they do not know, / in paths that they have not known I will guide them . . . These are the things I do.*[9] It seems God's modus operandi is to lead beyond retina and concha.

*

That darkness is fertile soil, ground for rooting in God. Conjuring my own light is dangerous. Isaiah:

> *Let him who walks in darkness . . .*
> *rely on his God.*
> *Walk by the light of your fire . . .*
> *you shall lie down in torment.*[10]

In her zeal to bring Psyche away from the mythic valley, Orual manipulates her sister into bringing forbidden light into her bedchamber and shining it on the face of her Beloved. The moment the light strikes him, a great flash lays the valley bare, tempest unleashed. Lightning illuminates falling trees and pillars and rock. The mountain itself breaks. When the Beloved arises, Orual's eyes cannot bear his terrible light. Soaked and startled, Psyche is forced into exile.[11]

I wonder if I really only want to know things (the next step, the right purchase, the heart behind the mask) for myself, to strengthen my independence—rather than to know God.

And yet God seeks to know me.

Not knowing draws me to the floorboards. I grapple for ground, for some kind of rock. God feels nearer here. Perhaps it is divine love that leads me into darkness. Perhaps God craves my nearness and redemption so much that he leads me through paths that press me to himself.

Darkness, then, can be a grace.

*

Still, I am a human with eyes. I seek divine signs I can hold within my vision. I want to be initiated into the secret rites of divine things, to see the face of the One Whom My Soul Loves—even if it's just a tormenting glimpse.[12] In the uncertain darkness of pregnancy, I want to hold dry wool and dew-sodden wool. Bright stars and post-flood rainbows.

Here are my own rainbows: The veins that curve into a blue heart on my breast. A forgotten heart fingered in the dust of my husband's car. The rock formation hewn into a heart.

In these three I hear a voice, and the voice calls, *Beloved*.

*

My poet-philosopher-bike mechanic father tells me what he's learning: it is more important to unlearn than to learn. To unknow.

Isaiah shatters my Sunday-school images of God (Though these images have their place, it may be that we underestimate what children, natural mythmakers, can hold with their

Cheerios and juice). *His lips are full of fury, / and his tongue is like a devouring fire; / his breath is like an overflowing stream that reaches up to the neck.*[13]

The images ascend to the mythic: *The LORD with his hard and great and strong sword will punish Leviathan the fleeing serpent, Leviathan the twisting serpent, and he will slay the dragon that is in the sea.*[14] This is the LORD of mountain-shattering storms, veiled in shadow, the One Who Hides Himself.

Like Psyche's Beloved, this God's face cannot be seen.

The God of Isaiah knows his own mysteriousness in human eyes: *For the LORD will rise up . . . to do his deed—strange is his deed! / and to work his work—alien is his work!*[15] He even obscures his messages: *And the vision of all this has become to you like the words of a book that is sealed.*[16]

I wonder if my blindness is rooted not in a lack of reading but a surfeit, if somehow I would see more clearly in space without human lights.

*

In my second trimester, my husband and I trek Yosemite for part of our babymoon. Here is what we do not have in the mountainous wilderness: our external brains called phones, voice-activated robots at our beck and call, light and water flowing with a flipped lever, a refrigerator so full as to be hazardous. My illusion of control.

At Cathedral Lake, we dip our toes in waters full of cloud and sky. Gray cliffs intricate as Gothic spires surround us. Ashy clouds amass about their summits, swallowing light.

This church is dark.

Soon gentle rain beckons us to gather our dusty shoes. Then the drops multiply beyond bearing, freeze into icy pebbles of hail, and we rush to the cover of trees we did not plant and cannot name. My city skin grows cold. I cannot remember the path. I think of the child resting in the dark of my womb.

Isaiah: *And the LORD will cause his majestic voice to be heard and the descending blow of his arm to be seen in furious anger and a flame of devouring fire, with a cloudburst and storm and hailstones.*[17]

I pray.

*

I pray to leave this dark, but what if I am called to remain here?

Mystics sing the gifts of darkness. It is not always a cauldron of judgment. The dark can be a gracious space for sojourners. As the Puritan prayer says, "the valley"—the place of Psyche's pillared home—"is the place of vision."[18]

And though we often want to speed through the valleys, the mystics tell us not to be afraid to stay there. The author of *The Cloud of Unknowing* encourages readers to remain in the cloud of darkness, in the space of unknowing, without recourse to rationality or easy emotional affection. "And therefore shape thee to bide in this darkness as long as thou mayest, evermore crying after him that thou lovest. For if ever thou shalt feel him or see him, as it may be here, it behoveth always to be in this cloud in this darkness."[19]

Here in the soul's night, says St. John of the Cross, we glimpse more of the abysses of our weakness, the infinite summits of the Most High. Understanding more of our own brokenness is a gift, though an excruciating one.[20] Here in newborn humility we can learn to love. Darkness is the secret chamber where God and the believer commune in the sweet intimacy of lovers.[21]

Merton, in a prayer before midnight mass at Christmas in 1941:

> Your brightness is my darkness.
> I know nothing of You and, by myself,
> I cannot even imagine how to go about knowing You.

If I imagine You, I am mistaken.
If I understand You, I am deluded.
If I am conscious and certain I know You, I am crazy.
The darkness is enough.[22]

*

It does not often feel like enough. With Orual I wonder, "Why must holy places be dark places?"[23]

At one of my appointments, an ultrasound reveals that one of my unborn child's kidneys is enlarged. Perhaps it is nothing. Perhaps it is serious. The tech cannot tell me. But she schedules another ultrasound with a specialist. How is it possible to be so intimately close to a being yet be so far away?

*

After the mountains have flowed with the blood of the know-it-alls. After the corpse-stench has risen like perverse incense. After the skies have been rolled up like a scroll, stars snuffed. After the streams have blackened to pitch. After the earth has crumbled to sulfur. After thorns have choked the strongholds.[24] *Then the eyes of those who see will not be closed, / and the ears of those who hear will give attention.*[25] After everything has become an emptiness, eyes and ears will grasp that the only certainty, the only solid being in existence, the only omniscient one is God.

*

Recently, I've been ruminating on intentional ignorance, intentionally giving up the quest for omniscience incited by instantaneous news and media and screen-barriered connections. Pelleted with continuous information, the margin of our perceived uncertainty diminishes while the margin of our perceived power inflates. Certainty becomes an opioid. These are soul-shaping habits.

To believe I can hold all knowledge is not only an illusion—it is dangerous. And simply exhausting. I do not want to blindfold myself or inoculate myself with easy fantasies. But I know my finite brain and body and soul cannot hold much. I try to intentionally remain ignorant of friends from past seasons in order to be more present with those in the season I'm in. To not scroll through the headlines in order to better hold my husband's story of a long day. Even David writes of intentional unknowing in one of my favorite Psalms:

> O LORD, my heart is not lifted up;
>   my eyes are not raised too high;
> I do not occupy myself with things
>   too great and too marvelous for me.
> But I have calmed and quieted my soul,
>   like a weaned child with its mother;
> like a weaned child is my soul within me.
>   O Israel, hope in the LORD
> from this time forth and forevermore.[26]

*

After the specialist's ultrasound, my husband and I know our child's kidneys are fine. But by intention, we do not know our child's sex. My mother said there is nothing like that moment in the delivery room when the doctor guides the baby from the womb and says, "It's a boy!" or "It's a girl!" My husband said there are so few genuine surprises in life, and he wanted this to be one.

There is a certain thrill in not knowing: a romance and mystery rich with whiffs of Poirot's puzzling or the tantalizing chase between Pip and Estella or Orual's search for exiled Psyche. This darkness is pregnant with possibilities: within that cloudy space anything could be; the imagination unreels, wild and unbound.

There is a kind of hopefulness to the dark.

The excommunicated mystic Meister Eckhart speaks of the need to give up the senses, every natural faculty for discernment, to truly see a God beyond all comprehension.[27] If I choose to unknow God, God becomes infinite and elusive and wild. God becomes something I cannot begin to grasp. When I hush my heart and listen and scrape all of the words and images of God I know out of my brain, what is left is a void pulsing with a power more formidable than I could have ever imagined.

*

I imagine the secret happenings within my womb. The divine and my unborn at play. God gently elongating the spine, the fingers, the toes, tucking the eyes and ears in their proper places. I imagine the sweet labor of an artist at play, an artist who has forgotten himself in the joy of creating. I imagine God humming as he works, even though he knows he is forming a body seeded with the capacity for every kind of evil.[28] I imagine God spinning the gauze and gold of the soul, breathing spirit with his lips like a flutist whispering a precise note.

Beyond eye and ear is a reality that makes our dusty world seem dreamlike by comparison. Describing her home in the valley, Psyche says it is "something new, never conceived of."[29]

There is much I do not see, but I believe it is much grander—and terrifying—than I could ever grasp.

*

Utterly uninitiated, my husband and I didn't know what to expect on our trip to Yosemite. In this mythic playground, I feel like a child seeing bubbles for the first time, trembling by the cliffs overlooking the valley, the rock cheeks of El Capitan. Dizzied by the free fall of waters, the weight of gravity in the waters of Vernal Falls as they rush over the edge of the cliff into the boulders below. I am reminded of the verses in Ezekiel and the Apocalypse: *And I heard a voice from heaven like the roar of many waters.*[30]

Perhaps the most poignant moment unfolds when we descend from Cathedral Lake into Tuolumne Meadows at sunset. Dark clouds glower over the mountain to the east while the sun sings unadulterated in the west. A glistening, easy rain glitters as we eat our simple dinner under the branches of a very old tree. Deer gather to feast in the grasses. And against the darkness, a double rainbow. I feel I have stumbled into some kind of other world. A tear in the veil.

*

Near the end of her life, Orual has a dream (or is it real?) of discovering walls painted in stories. Here at last are answers to questions that have strangled Orual for most of her life. The images reveal that exiled Psyche had to descend into the Deadlands to wrest beauty from the Queen of Shadows. That Psyche was present, bearing Orual's own anguish in times of dark distress. God is as close as a newborn swaddled in a mother's womb.

"I know now, Lord, why you utter no answer," Orual says in the last paragraph of her story. "You are yourself the answer. Before your face questions die away."[31]

*

Perhaps in heaven the divine will be a volcanic cloud, a ferocious dark that gives birth to every color, to light. Or perhaps this side of the veil, God's caustic brightness burns our eyes blind, that divine light is so bright it seems dark. Perhaps all of our senses are mistuned, to one day be upended, upset in a sudden clash, a rush of thunder and bloody pangs and the clanging of everything broken and restored.

Fluorescent lights and excruciating tears and an emptied womb and a cry singing for the first time in the history of the universe.

*

Talking with my sister about Yosemite, I tell her of the freedom I feel in those wide spaces. Cluttered cities choke; but in the west, there are spaces to breathe. She, another sister, and my nephew have already moved out to Denver to be near sun and mountains. They are adept at gathering the unknown into their souls and cherishing it.

In the midst of the pandemic and the mourning of national racial injustices, my brother and his wife also sought refuge in the west that summer, as did my parents and youngest sister, as did my husband and I. There is something liberating, something healing here.

"Maybe that's why wilderness is so freeing," my sister says. "We realize we're not in control."

And then I imagine the dark woods, spun with the blue song of streams, and I am spinning under the light-struck leaves, dancing in pockets of wildflowers, knowing the rest that comes from releasing everything into strong hands I cannot see.

holy houseflies:

on

annoyances

We must be ready to allow ourselves to be interrupted by God, who will thwart our plans and frustrate our ways time and again, even daily.

—Deitrich Bonhoeffer, Life Together

My house is cool and ordered. As I write, the spoons are stacked in their fitted bamboo tray. I've polished the grooves in the silver sink handles with a toothbrush. Autumn has stayed the blades of grass and mower. Dry towels and socks fill the loveseat, but I have time to fold each piece as neatly as I'm folding this day into a pocket square.

Yet.

These quiet hours will soon thrum with a new voice. My husband and I expect a baby in a swift blur of months. My edifice of right angles and scrubbed corners will soon unfold.

*

Over plastic bowls of quick noodles, my friend and I discuss children. She never wanted to be a mother. Her small son won't stop talking, and her even smaller daughter whips out sass like a switchblade. "If I could just have the house to myself," my friend sighs. "Just a few hours to chill at the kitchen table in my underwear." I nod. I, too, covet my quiet.

It seems in my small circles that children are often viewed as annoyances. Cries that cut through sleep. Bottomless drains on cash and crackers. The beginning of the end of marital intimacy, those little bodies wriggling between mom and dad in the bed. Dreams of paying off the house in five years, of traveling to anywhere on a whim, of becoming that elusive true self—gone. Children like flies hovering over the roast, table set like a Dutch still life.

*

My theology of children is nascent but firm on a few points: Children are a divine gift created in the image of God, their presence a reward. As children multiply, so do blessings. Children are not annoyances to be smacked with a fly swatter or a dismissive hand. But I know I will find aspects of childrearing irksome, irritating. Annoying. Now is the time to develop a theology of annoyances. Quotidian life provides plenty of practice.

*

For teachers like myself trapped in COVID-induced virtual learning, annoyances abound. I miss the beautiful and exhausting energy of human beings tucked into a common space for a common purpose. I miss the opportunity to discern expressions, to touch a troubled shoulder. To press my pencil to the paper, identify the problem with a tap. To look someone in the eyes.

In this virtual sphere unbound in many ways by physical restraint, I am frustrated. My Zoom screen freezes in the middle of the period, and I have to restart my computer, plunge our illusory classroom into darkness. Students can't open files, lose all their careful edits, can't find the video I posted, disappear from class in a gust of faulty internet. Flies settle on my skin, and I shiver like a mare in a summer field.

*

I read that flies nourish swallows and kingbirds, frogs and turtles, chickens and wasps. Flies do the labor no one else wants to do. They clean up carcasses and manure, transforming rot into nourishment for the earth, for green growing things, and eventually for my dinner plate. They pollinate flowers the bees have snubbed: the nectarless ones, the drab ones dressed in dull tones, the ones that stink. Those unsightly hairs on blow flies allow them to carry more pollen than honey bees. Without the midges to pollinate the cacao tree, I wouldn't be able to savor my tiny squares of bitter chocolate.

*

One thing I learned from the '90s sitcom *Seinfeld* is that much of this pendular, ponderous life hinges on the small things. Great spiritual dramas of the human soul—sword fights with anger and selfishness, crucial choices to overlook an offense or amplify it—unfold in the realm of seeming minutiae: the low talkers and trouble ordering soup. The children refusing to swallow the peas and the spouse refusing to use the hamper. The drafty Zoom calls and the broken zipper and the kale in the teeth. Perhaps annoyances are as much what they are in themselves as my perspective towards them. Flies as part of a process of transformation.

And I need that.

*

Sometimes I crave the physicality of unordered desks and the tissue box empty again. Funny how I can see these annoyances from another life with fondness. They were woven intrinsically into that other, physical world. They were signs of breathless, disorderly life (only what is dead is perfectly still). The endless need to sweep Goldfish crumbs, to scrub broiler pans, to wash sweat-ringed shirts roots in the glorious gift of life itself.

I attempt this prayer: *thank you, Lord, for it all, all that I am living here and now.* It is all part of this life, this present life.

*

My mother calls at the end of the day, one of those brutal back-to-school days. After school, I've been walking to sort through the burdens that subtly accumulate until five or six or seven in the evening, that settle in painful creases in my shoulders and fingers and mind. I am almost home. I've been planning out the rest of the evening, ordering my minutes from the moment my feet will press the living-room floor. If my evening were a still life (or dead nature, *nature morte*, as the French say), it would include my soft indigo robe and the novel I've just started.

I sigh. My mother's call is unexpected, a kink in my therapeutic plans. I let the phone ring a few times, deciding whether to allow the interruption.

Whether by filial obligation or acquiescence to the Spirit, I say hello. My mother asks about my day, shares her own. She is calling just to say hi, just to say she loves me.

What if I had not welcomed her in conversation? If I had not embraced what I saw as annoyance? I would have silenced a voice, precisely ordered it seems to me now, to encourage me after a difficult day.

A voice reminding me I was loved.

*

My father says that losing things is a gentle nudge to pause and rest, an indication of too many piled plans and a soul disordered. Another bit of paternal advice: keep the keys in a designated drawer.

*

Of course, not all annoyances have discernable, neatly drawn blessings or fill-in-the-blank lessons I can summarize with a few words and a smile. Either I am too blind to see the good in my car battery dying for the third time in three days, or annoying can be just plain annoying.

Bob Dylan singing "everything is broken" somehow unconstricts my heart a few notches. The Preacher's hum that all is vanity unclenches a kind of hope.[1] Perhaps because these words are true, and truth liberates. Yes, the battery is broken, as everything else seems to be.

None of the dropped Zoom calls and vanished Google Docs should be a surprise. I think my life might be much less stressful if I lived with this kind of expectation. Perhaps instead of being easily miffed, I should be easily amazed: grateful that anything right happens at all. This, the gift of good in a world abuzz with evil, is the true anomaly. These are some of those clean new mercies weeping Jeremiah sings of.[2]

The dust on the shelf and the ink on the cuff, the missing charger and the dead bulb all remind me earth is no kind of heaven.

*

I need that fly sizzle in my ears.

Monastics seek out annoyance and discomfort for the purpose of self-mortification: the itchy clothing of animal hair, the metal prongs of a cilice pressing against thighs, bodies bound in wire, sleeping in snow.

All sound rather morbid to my low-church Protestant ears. Yet those who practice self-mortification say this is not a masochistic practice, pain for its own sake. It is intentionally embodying Christ's passion, denying oneself to cultivate sacrificial love. To actively struggle against the god of personal comfort.

Take this portrait: slabs of overpriced cake fitted in tailored, pale pink boxes. When I open mine, I am annoyed by the stinginess of the slice, the dryness of the crumb. Stale. I cannot enjoy it. Like I can't enjoy the evening when a TV show won't load or when my husband carefully articulates his seminary musings at the precise moment I would rather be alone in a story. So many flies. So much unearthed pettiness.

I don't think I will slip a cilice under my skirt anytime soon. But I do wonder what would happen if I saw daily annoyances as little goads to remember what I was not made for, and what I was.

*

If I was not so selfish, could I be annoyance-proof? I recall the book of James. The fights (with others, yes, and within oneself?) buzz because of wrong desires.[3] Desires for personal pleasures. My couch. My cookie. My cup of tea. My demands for neat shelves and ironed collars which all too often supersede the divine whispers to call my aging Nana or to simply uncurl in the presence of a God who longs just to be with me.

I pray to desire different things. To know what to desire at all.

*

Funny how flies often settle on the reeking and rotting. In one of his letters, poet and theologian François Fénelon writes that if we were really dead to certain sins, we wouldn't feel pain when they were cut off. "The more acutely we feel, the more certainly we know that the correction was necessary."[4] Perhaps those same places that make me shudder with fly-itch are the same parts of myself that need to die: the gluttonous craving for cake and the impatience to entertain myself numb. Like teachers' fingers, the flies are tapping on the places that need restoration. Maybe in this way, they are a kind of hairy illumination, a grace.

God knows what we need, and we need these flies. Needed: the interrupting phone call and the grumpy internet and the airplane's middle seat and the burnt coffee and the way that he chews with his mouth askew (these signs of thrumming life). Flies, bulbous eyes and all, undertaking the labor of sanctification no one else wants to handle.

*

And yet.

God may need to teach me patience through burnt coffee, but it's not to say I have to try and burn it next time. If we are little Christs, we are called to right what is wrong in the world.⁵ It's a tricky balance, this: practicing self-renunciation yet refusing the yokes of our own devising, acquiescing to this life lived through a veil and laboring to tear the veil down.

*

It seems many of my daily annoyances root in my own assessment of what I need. I have vigorously constructed my schedule to reflect these needs, mostly to finish tasks in enough time to take a quiet walk or still myself in bath bubbles at the end of the day—alone. But perhaps what I need are the tics and smacks and jabs from human elbows around me: people.

Often I naively make my schedule to suit one (me). And that does not work in a world of humans. It does not work in a marriage. It will not work with children. How absurd and selfish to uphold the expectation that my still little life can cleanly synthesize with those of others and to blame them for bumping my bubble, the iridescent wonder easily popped into a sticky glob on the floor.

My hours are not my own.

*

One of the oddities of being pregnant is that people enjoy touching your burgeoning belly. These foreign hands on my body and my baby bother me. I shoo them away.

Ancient Middle-Eastern personal boundaries certainly differ from my contemporary Middle-American ones, but I still wonder at Jesus's response to embodied human interruption. The harried mothers pushing their children forward, begging for a touch. The lepers lurking in the street, odious in rag and stench. A demon-possessed naked man haunting a cemetery. The poorly planned wedding when the wine ran out. Over five thousand hungry people who hadn't the forethought to pack a lunch. People poking prayers upward at all hours of the day and night.

And this: in the jumble of sweaty bodies, dust in the sandal crevices, a hundred voices knotted together in a buzzing swarm—a bleeding woman grasps the fringe of Jesus's mantle. How simple to ignore the tug on the hem, to shrug off that annoying, subtle slowing.

But the One Who Holds All Things pauses.

So sensitive, so gentle, Jesus has felt her. Deeply. A departing rush of power flows towards the grip of the fraught fingers.

He calls her *daughter*.

It seems that we humans who bleed and break are far from annoying interruptions. But the very substance of Jesus's life, and the call of my own.[6]

*

This story reminds me of Deitrich Bonhoeffer's thoughts on when God sends demanding, needy people across our path:

> We can, then, pass them by, preoccupied with our important daily tasks, just as the priest—perhaps reading the Bible—passed by the man who had fallen among robbers. When we do that, we pass by the visible sign of the Cross raised in our lives to show us that God's way,

and not our own, is what counts . . . It is a strange fact that Christians and even ministers frequently consider their work so important and urgent that they will allow nothing to disturb them. They think they are doing God a service in this, but actually they are disdaining God's "crooked yet straight path."7

*

After a full day burning my eyes on a laptop screen. Attempting to gather human voices from the void of blank black boxes. To create conversation in ether. After saying over and over again, *could you unmute yourself—could you turn on your video—could you raise your hand—could you share your screen—could you work with me here?* I am ready to hide under the quiet drudgery of administration. But as usual, at least one student lags behind. I normally ask if they have questions, and if not, I go or hint that they should with a syrupy "*Au revoir.*"

The Spirit whispers, *Stay.* I try the crooked yet straight path. "*Bonjour, ça va?*" I ask. I am resting my head in the cup of my hand.

"*Ça va,*" he says. I want to ask my perfunctory "*As-tu des questions?*" and then leave. But I remember he had mentioned going to a September 11th memorial in Pennsylvania. The Spirit nudges. I ask about his visit.

"It was good, but sad, you know," he says. He shares how one of his mom's friends died in the crash. "It's one thing to watch all that on TV, but it's like so different actually being there."

Actually being there. Being there in the physical space of suffering, beyond the veil of screens. Mourning together in close proximity to sniffles and snot, hiccups and the sounds of weeping.

Being there.

*

If my narrow schedule is shattered, that harsh-angled temple, then I am free. Free to bend with a time not my own, to sway lithe and limber with the Spirit. If I did not create or earn the hours I inhabit, they are not mine. In releasing my *chronos* minutes and months, I enter into the time outside time, the endless, holy moment of *kairos* beyond the veil.[8]

How often do the prophets say, *Listen?* Listen and live, or the way will be lost. I wonder what would happen if I gave as much energy to listening and moving with God as I do to designing my personal planner. The thought unnerves me. But also awes with a sense of unboundedness, a spacious liberty. The divine yoke is light.

*

Here is what I pray for: Grace to give up the pocket squares. Eyes to see beauty in tumbling and spatter and things undone—so much ineffable life. A body and a spirit light enough to move easy with divine winds.

That such a dance would be enough.

*

Here is what I imagine in a few months: pillows in the kitchen and tiny, dirty socks in the yard. I imagine novels left mid-sentence or not picked up at all. I imagine guests showing up before the noodles are boiled, jelly gluing bills to the counter. Swatting away the fly that escaped in through an open door, and laughing.

jet skis in a storm:

on fear

All the familiar land looks as though it were not solid and real at all, but painted on a scroll like a backdrop, and that unrolled scroll has been shaken, so the earth sways and the air roars.

—Annie Dillard, "Flood," Pilgrim at Tinker Creek

P ositive.
I can't be positive.

My husband Dagi and I sit tense, at opposite corners of our bed, the gray-blue comforter between us tousled like stormy seas. We have just opened the results of our COVID tests.

I can't be positive. I am almost forty weeks pregnant with our first child. Pregnant women are more likely to require hospitalization, ICU admission, medical ventilation.[1] Their babies are more at risk for preterm birth, infection, death.[2] If I am positive, there's a chance Dagi could become positive too, unable to stand beside me during our child's birth. I imagine myself in the delivery room, trembling with the most intense agony of my life, wheezing through a mask—alone.

It is one of those moments—bone-jittery, soul-lurching—when it feels like everything stable and solid melts into a slippery pool, or a wild sea you could drown in. When the floor and ceiling somehow shift places. When the mountain peaks, the most secure thing you can think of, sink into ocean foam.[3]

*

My pandemic pregnancy—and subsequent COVID infection—forced me to reckon with fear. At the time, little was known about the virus in the first place, let alone its particular dangers to pregnant women and their unborn children. Perhaps it was the gaping unknown—the very invisibility of a global, killing threat I could not measure—which, more than anything else, unsettled.

I armored myself with a film of face mask, clipped a little bottle of hand sanitizer to my purse, wiped down cartons of eggs from the grocery store, kept the windows ajar.

Avoided hugs. When a dear friend I hadn't seen in weeks slipped into our home for tea, she eyed my burgeoning womb, entering lightly as if the floor itself were fragile. I did not move forward to embrace her. Wallflower-like, she sensed the imposed distance, kept herself tethered to the space where a welcome mat should be.

*

Fear incites me to protect what is valuable, namely, life. But fear can also destroy life. This is where it grays, this line between caution and fear, between wisdom and paranoia, between dancing the steps of life and falling like a fool.

Driving to my baby shower, I still haven't decided whether to hug people or not. My generous hosts have taken precautions: the event will be outside despite the threat of October chill; people have been told to wear masks; only one person will serve the egg bake and apple crisp; a bottle of hand sanitizer will sit beside the carafes of decaf coffee and cider.

After parking, I walk the gravel drive to the backyard but hear a call behind me. It is my friend of nearly twenty years, the one who dared to sit next to me in the back row at youth group. We have lamented boys on her rooftop, eaten chocolate chip cookie dough raw in bowls, accumulated years of penpal letters. Before my mind can fence me behind precaution, before bee-like fear can sting, a deeper kind of instinct has bent my body into a gripping embrace.

Within the arms of my friend, I feel something beyond safe: loved.

*

My parents erred on the side of dancing through life. My father would take us children out to the porch during reckless storms and teach us to delight in the pulse of thunder. When a deep snow swallowed the roads one Christmas morning, the kind of snowfall that cancels schools and karate classes and church services, my parents didn't hesitate to drive to Grandma's house, albeit slowly.

Once, my parents took us jet-skiing onto the massive wilderness of Lake Michigan. After we had skidded out into far deeps we could not fathom, the sky began to shadow darker and pricks of rain stung our skin. Before we could return to the weather-worn docks, feral winds scooped giant waves out of the waters. Our little arms clung to our parents' life jackets as we rose and fell with the lake's whims: an untamed roller coaster. I sensed an almost mythic power in the waters, a virulence that could crush children's bones. My little sisters began to cry.

My parents later lamented their foolishness. (Would I lament the baby-shower hugs? Would I regret the exchange of three seconds of lovely closeness for the risk of weeks—or months, years—of a danger I could not grasp?)

But I did not cry. Not because I was a particularly brave child. In fact, I was profoundly shy and often couldn't sleep for fear of kidnappers and divorce and fire. My mother had to force me to jump off the diving board for the first time. (And when I did, I discovered a whole new dimension of pleasure.)

I think in those moments when the impenetrable gray waves bulked into towers and free-fell into caverns, when I moved, helpless, with muscular motions so beyond me, what I felt more than terror, was wonder.

*

Maybe fear and wonder are not so different; or perhaps wonder is a kind of fear, a good kind. Wonder seems rooted in an awareness, acceptance, and even delight in human smallness before magnificence. Or rather, in wonder our smallness is forgotten, inundated, in the joy and awe of something wildly grand.

In wonder, life angles into perspective. My candy-floss ego dissolves as I realize I am not the universe-centering goddess of my illusions. My problems and pet peeves diminish in the presence of a grandeur that arrests my rhythmic intake of oxygen. (Even survival, it seems, bows before the presence of the awesome.) I see, for a second, my "almost infinite fragility," as Simone Weil describes it.[4] And beyond myself, I see, for a second, the reality of God, and my deepest purpose: to worship him.

One summer during university, I trekked into Switzerland with a fresh passport, alone. A daughter of the cornfield-flat Midwest, I was accustomed to lands reaching no higher than sledding hills. I hiked to an overlook perched before an Alpine panorama, gaped.

Behold!

That muscular blue power shouting all kinds of praises. Those fortressing arms of rock. The snow-tipped ridges I feared falling from, even from my perch far away. Before those peaks, I felt a peculiar and wonderful weakness, a giving way, a sweet unsettling. My tidy rhythms of easy breath fell out of order. Then, tears. (And later, when I showed my patient family hundreds of photographs from my journey, this moment, even experienced second-hand through the veil of screens and space, brought some to tears, too.)

Delightful discombobulation. Delight in the reality of a power beyond me. (What a relief that my life is not dependent on my own weak hands.) Delight in the reality of transcendent beauty. Delight in the discovery of an expanse, a dimension of the world, wholly new to me, unveiled as it were for the first time.

*

Delight—and yet—unsettling. Floating on the comically small jet-ski over monstrous Lake Michigan, I gripped my daddy as tightly as I could. Tension surely constricted my chest, breath, as I imagined everyone in my family drowning and wondered if we would make it to the wind-eaten docks again. Maybe this is part of the delight of the Alps, too, that those heartless arms of rock could destroy my earthly body. Maybe this is part of why some people like roller coasters and peering over the Grand Canyon's edge. Being out of your depth, acknowledging that a few more inches forward could be the end—creates a certain thrill.

Here is fear again as a kind of shepherding force: *come back from the edge, child.* My father ushered us into thunderstorms, but kept us tucked under the wings of the porch. During my pandemic pregnancy, I hid my nose and mouth behind home-sewn fabric. Some kinds of power must be engaged from a distance.

Maybe wonder forms the basis for a nourishing fear of God.

*

If my sister hadn't already chosen the name for her son, I might have named our first boy Moses. Moses feared. At the burning bush, thrilling and terrifying wonder, he doubts himself:[5] *Who am I that I should go?* He fears people will question his legitimacy: *Who should I say sent me?* Despite divine answers, he continues to doubt, and God gives him two signs and the promise of a third (besides, of course, the burning bush): the staff morphing into a snake, his hand shifting from whole to leprous and back again in an instant. And still this is insufficient.

I am not eloquent, Moses says, *I am slow of speech and tongue.* He is so shy God gives him Aaron to speak on his behalf. I wonder if God chose him precisely for these reasons. I wonder if God placed Moses in a situation that would bring him nose-to-nose with his deepest fears, that would push him free-falling into his own abysmal need.

What strikes me is how Moses's fear engages him in a dialogue with God. God does not condemn Moses's doubt. God knows the strength and frailty of the dust he has formed in his own image. Instead, God meets Moses in conversation.

Fear can awaken engagement with the divine.

I think of the car ride to the baby shower, my repeated prayers for wisdom, orienting my heart heavenward. How my uncertainty and need led me into conversation with God. And then after the baby shower, I prayed for protection for myself, my unborn child, every soul that sat in the circle of chairs upon the grass and showered me with bags and boxes of blessings.

My fears push me into prayer.

*

Perhaps it is not fear that is sinful, but remaining in fear. Perhaps the challenge is to let fear lead to faith.

What faith Moses would have shown had trust arisen and not terror! What if Moses had trusted God from the moment he heard the ageless voice within the glowing bush, confident of a holy presence to guide him? Would he have ascended into deeper levels of communion with God had his initial reaction been faith? I can only imagine.

For my own sake, I am thankful for Moses's flaws, for they encourage me in my own. Moses would have saved himself great anxiety if he had chosen to trust first instead of tremble; but I am encouraged by how God redeems Moses's faltering heart. God gathers the pieces of Moses's fear and recreates them into a beautiful dance of conversation, towards deeper knowing, deeper intimacy, with the divine.

*

This past week after dinner on the porch, as the autumnal dark fell over our empty plates, I moved to go back inside, to the light and warmth. My husband's voice stopped me. "I wasn't sure if I should tell you this or not. I didn't want to worry you."

Immediately, something fell heavy in my stomach, breath thrown off, and my mind began to conjure a series of fears: somebody was sick, somebody was unfaithful, somebody died. I paused, silent, alert as a squirrel sensing human footfall.

My husband said he was turning left from his office's parking lot onto the rushing road. He looked to the right, but assumed the left was clear. Seeing an open slot in the traffic, he began to gun the gas, when he felt a divine nudge to stop. The van careening towards him braked aggressively, swerving into the other lane.

My husband was moments, inches, from a head-on collision.

How often do my husband and I eat dinner and all I can think about is how tired I am? As the darkness and the cool deepened on the porch, I realized our dinner together was a great gift. That my husband came home was no ordinary grace, but a divine deliverance. That my child will have a father is not granted. So much of what I fear I cannot anticipate. It jumps from the shadows, freakish and unreal. I rose and gripped my husband's body, felt the edges of his dusk-lit muscles, pressed my nose into his neck.

Fear shows you what, who, you love.

*

I love control far too much. In my goddess moods, I fear the chaos ensuing if the pillows are not angled just so on the couch. I fear not having enough food for tomorrow when my husband eats not one helping of crock-pot chicken but two. I fear any shape of harm coming to my family and friends, fear them making unexpected moves—anything that would jerk my breathing out of order.

But I never can keep the pillows straight. Viruses hide phantom-like in the air. Two of my sisters and my little nephew Moses moved to mountainous Denver. A dear family friend just decided to go off the feeding tube: a small act of independence in the rock-face of a cancer that has taken away most of his earthly decisions.

Years ago, I would pray that my sisters wouldn't move away. My prayers were more specific then. I prayed what I wanted over the people I loved (mostly as it related to my own perceived well-being). I still do this, but less as I begin to understand more of the awesome love of God—the Alp-expansive, wave-roaring kind that leaves my body and soul in a jittery joy, undone.

*

When God engages Moses in the conversational dance before the flames, God does not try to build him up with some kind of self-help psychobabble: *You can do this! You are a mighty warrior! Believe in yourself!*

Quite the opposite. God shifts Moses's focus from his own human weakness to the power of God: Look up to the

God of the wild waters and the God of the Alps and the God of a bush that burns but is not consumed. God says, *I will be with you.* God proves Godself with mini-miracles right there in the eternal firelight and promises more. God says who God is: I AM, the self-existent one, the breath in your body. Moses's very uncertainty throws God's power into awesome relief.

Relief, that feeling when I release my tight-wound prayers, which is to say, release my illusory and exhausting grip on the universe: when I learn trust in a fiery, wild, and gracious power that demands awe.

*

I am still learning to pray this way. I am still learning to fear the right One rather than the wrong things. Encounters with God (the bush aflame) and encounters with evil (the positive COVID test) both discombobulate. But only God is worthy of fear.

Lately I've been reading the book of Jeremiah, a prophet who, like Moses, wrestled in conversation with God about his fear of speaking up.[6] Prophesying of divine judgment, Jeremiah says:

> The sound of a cry comes from Babylon,
> And great destruction from the land of the Chaldeans,
> Because the LORD is plundering Babylon
> And silencing her loud voice,
> Though her waves roar like great waters,
> And the noise of their voice is uttered.[7]

Shifting my feet into the sandals of the Babylonians, I imagine my worst fears becoming rock-hard reality: loss of my daily routine as a teacher, loss of my bank accounts, loss of my bungalow in Indianapolis, loss of my little books and bowls. Loss of my country, loss of my fists, loss of my immune system, loss of any kind of defense (as if my puny attempts at self-armoring amount to anything in the face of a wrathful God). And here is where it gets unbearably difficult: loss of my community, my family, my husband, my child. Loss of everything on earth I consider strong and immovable: trustworthy. Drowned in bone-crushing waves.

If I can hold my hope in my hands, I am always in danger of losing it.

*

It was during a prayer for my sisters, before they both moved away.

Perhaps I was pressing my knees into the hardwood floors, hands clasped in the morning silence that hovers before daytime rumbles to life. Or perhaps I'm slicing onions for dinner or making a left-hand turn onto our street. I'm not sure what shifted in my spirit, what changed.

What is certain: the settling and unsettling release, hard-fought grace, when I prayed the words, *Thy will be done.*

*

As it turns out, God's will was to heal me of COVID, just days before I gave birth. My husband stood beside me as a doctor wrestled a wriggling baby from my body. Crouched before that miracle, I wondered like Moses before the flaming leaves.

*

On Lake Michigan, I moved with the wind-gouged waves. Now I pray to move with accidents and farewells and illness. This is not a fatalistic limpness in the face of earthly brokenness. I pray, *Deliver us from evil* just as I pray, *Thy will be done.* I pray for healing though I know to the world it is foolishness. I engage God in conversation, hurl my doubts and fears heaven-ward. I pray God will change his mind.

Yet I am learning the shape of a peace that trusts not in the power of the waves, but in a greater power that holds them the way a mother's hands cup her baby's face.

a long and chilly vigil:

on winter

Winter is not the death of the life cycle, but its crucible.

—Katherine May, Wintering

I am re-begot / Of absence, darkness, death: things which are not.

—John Donne, "A Nocturnal upon St. Lucy's Day, Being the Shortest Day"

Here is what I see. A sunless sky muffled in seamless clouds: one drape of gray. Penciled branches clutching at the heavens. Sidewalks strewn with skins of fallen leaves. A cold rain gives everything the appearance of drooping.

Seasonal affective disorder pushed my sisters from our hometown of Indianapolis to sunny Denver. It's why most members of my immediate family take vitamin D supplements between November and March. It explains why the shortest month of the year can feel the longest. My journal entries for winter months bear dark musings.

And yet.

This is all I can see. I take comfort in believing there is much I do not see; I take comfort in acknowledging my own blindness.

*

Perhaps part of the challenge of this season is training my eyes to see better. Winter beauty is not often obvious, hides darkly. On daily walks, I challenge myself to look beyond strutting blooms and fleshy fruit.

Against the emptied trees, I see cardinal flash. I see the sycamore's dappling white. I see sunbright clarify the world in its fading. I see canal waters mirroring forest fringe back to itself, as if saying that the trees, in all their bareness, are worthy of reflection.

Mornings I open the window blinds even though it is dark. On clear days, I watch as the dome blends from indigo to cobalt to azure to periwinkle to the finest watercolor blue. And sometimes, God peppers dashes of fiery rose and violet that force me to stand before the kitchen window and gawk at majesty.

*

But what if the skies are clouded, like today? I realize I may even have to change the definition of what I perceive to be beautiful. Could this be beauty: the black web of denuded branches, the thousand dun shades of dying leaves, how the birds shiver flecks of rain off their feathers?

Or maybe I am trying too hard. It may be that winter can look just plain ugly. That winter has truth, more than beauty, to reveal (though these two are tightly bound). That it is this very barrenness that makes sightings of the beautiful of infinitely more value.

*

In 2020, more than any other year, Christmas lights felt necessary. It's the year COVID shuttered the globe, the year Beirut exploded, the year of 53,000 wildfires, the year of so many tropical storms meteorologists exhausted their list of official names, the year of the Trump-Biden elections, the year the world erupted with raised fists after American police killed yet another and another black human being, the year my friend Cathy lost her husband to cancer, the year my Grandpa died.

One morning, I forgot to turn off the string of colored bulbs we'd wrapped around our tallest shrub, and on an afternoon walk I realized that I could scarcely tell if the lights were even on. So much vain light.

It is only when the darkness snuffs the winter sun, when the cold is coldest, that the lights sparkle like a crazed kind of hope.

*

In *The Cloister Walk*, poet Kathleen Norris recounts her experiences living at a Benedictine monastery, a beautifully bare world stripped to the rhythms of prayer, work, and Scripture. She asks, "If scarcity makes things more precious, what does it mean to choose the spare world over one in which we are sated with abundance . . . does living in [the spare world] bring with it certain responsibilities? Gratitude for example? The painful acceptance that underlies Psalm 16's 'happy indeed whatever heritage befalls me?'"[1]

*

My mom has a gift for naming beauty most people overlook. Snowfall makes her gleeful like a child. She still recounts releasing our childhood mutt into the snow, how he would dance in the powder with an unfettered joy, how he was, she says, glorifying God. In the mornings, she gasps at how the windows frame feathery works of frost-art.

And this: in winter, after a good snowfall, on a cloudless day, the sunlight reverberating off the snow and the ice and the frost—a massive echo chamber of luminosity, so bitingly bright you can hardly see.

*

In going back, I can learn to see winter differently. I can learn from my child-self, which as Madeleine L'Engle reminds, is part of who I am and always will be.[2] To walk whole into the future, we must seek a garden innocence that once was.

At the first snow, we children would glory in the miracle of numberless unique crystals—prisms, dendrites, rosettes, stars—descending like fine glitter from heaven. The snowfall heralded months of cold and cloudiness, yet I felt such joy: a deep, expansive release. As a child, all I saw was the sudden white like raining manna, a gift beyond me, one that covered all the world as I saw it.

Here is a litany my adult-self must recall:

Printing snow angels on the earth.

Whisking down sledding hills.

Hot chocolate ladled from the stovetop.

Standing over the heating vent as warmth ballooned my flannel nightgown.

Ice-skating.

Snowball skirmishes.

Running so hard I'd have to shed my puffy coat.

And how warm the fire felt after returning home in sodden socks.

*

My child eyes were keen to spot and relish wonder. In *Wintering*, Katherine May writes, "Snow creates that quality of awe in the face of a power greater than ours. It epitomises the aesthetic notion of the sublime, in which greatness and beauty couple to overpower you—a small, frail human—entirely."[3] As a child well-acquainted with my smallness (indeed, I was the smallest girl in my class for many years), I could better receive the awe-ful gift of snowfall. To acknowledge its magic.

Many novels and fairy tales unfold in snow.[4] The Pevensies step through the wardrobe into a white-trimmed forest and leave as kings and queens of a green summer realm. Elves cobble shoes for a hapless shoemaker in the winter dark, and his poverty transforms into a happily-ever-after abundance. Snow White's tale begins in midwinter, tucked in her mother's womb, and ends in resurrection.

Winter, the season of enchanted transformation hidden under ice-glitter and frost-lace, is a magical season. Beneath the shimmering veil of snow, animal hearts beat, fallen leaves nourish forest floors, new buds gestate. Winter is a silent herald announcing that someday, after a long and chilly vigil, something wonderful is going to happen.

*

Of course, winter does not always bode welcome change. It can be disastrous for some members of our human family. Enjoying snowfall from the comfort of a toasty living room is a privilege. Seven hundred homeless or at-risk homeless human beings die of hypothermia each year in the United States.[5] For my grandparents, slipping on a frozen puddle could mean broken bones and months, if not years, of recovery. Black ice can be deadly. To paint winter in purely jolly hues is naïve, ignoring the reality of human helplessness before nature's feral forces. The sublime's gift of unveiling our frailty thrills—and terrifies.

Terrifying: the reality that everyone—even those like me who don't often feel it—is vulnerable. The home I own and the relative youth I enjoy delude me into thinking I am stronger, more in control than I am. In one gust of icy wind, I could lose it all. In *Winter Solstice*, Nina MacLaughlin writes:

> Winter makes us know the hollows. Darkness creeps in from both sides and pushes us to that pure ridge, all the way exposed. Peer over. Scope the abyss. The fear is ancient and uncomplicated . . . will I be warm enough, will I have enough to eat, will the cold air reach my bones, will it keep getting darker, will the darkness swallow me, will it swallow us all together? Will I see spring?[6]

As the days shorten, I begin to feel the clutch of anxiety and not understand why. It takes time before I can consciously connect the slow dying of the sun to the despair that blooms in the dark.

Unsettled, I too often seek solace in frenetic distraction, pressing my gaze to text messages or emails or the ceaseless minutiae of social media. As if the illusion of action could banish the specter of sunless gloom.

But rather than shirk the abyss, what if we scoped its depths? What if we stared darkness in the face and saw, at that pure ridge, the truth of our essential finity? Like the begonias and the fallen leaves of wintertime, we will die.

We will die.

We will die.

Someday.

Though painful to receive, this knowledge is a gift. Embracing the reality of death sparks life. In winter's existential chill, we can feel, as MacLaughlin writes, "The temporary heat of our aliveness burning at its hottest."[7]

The heat is only temporary. Yes, we will die. But today we live. Now—in this flash of precious, precious time—we live.

We live.

We live.

Now.

In the face of inevitable death—the hollowed stalks, the still, still mornings, the green gone gray—we can acknowledge the life sparking in our bones. Heartbeats and breath unbidden, synapses sparking in a rhythm beyond our powers of control.

In short, utter grace.

*

Just as the winter-bitter illuminates the grace of being alive, it also offers opportunities for compassion. One evening of my adolescence, snow had left a moon-lit coat over the driveway and walks of our elderly neighbors, a tobacco-chewing farmer and his beautician-wife. I don't know how it started or who started it, but when my mom and I arrived at Joe and Linda's with snow shovels, we found ourselves working alongside other neighbors: Spanish-speaking Sal and the bald guy with the roaring Chevelle. We worked quietly as I recall, focused on clearing the patches of concrete before us. A gentle flurry of snow spun in the window light.

I remember feeling such joy. That this was what life was all about: this warm pocket of community sprung in the middle of the cold. That this was an important, and rare, moment. We finished quickly and returned to our homes.

*

Winter offers opportunities for compassion inside our homes as well. Instead of curling inwards towards screens, we can stretch our arms outwards to receive others. Cups of hot tea are all the warmer on cold days. A door opening to a well-lit living room can be a saving grace on dark nights. Even the hospitality of a smile opens a portal from the heavenly places where there is no night.

Just as human bodies must press together to survive places of inadequate heat and shelter, human hearts need the nearness of community, especially in winter's isolation. The chill draws us into essential intimacy. In the easy heat and fruit of summer, it is harder to realize not only our inherent fragility, but also our inherent need for each other. But winter's brutality—to divide, to uncover, to bury—opens our eyes to this beautiful fact.

Several years ago, I watched the documentary *Finding Hygge*, which explores the Danish art of finding coziness and joy, particularly in the midst of Nordic cold. The film helped inspire me to embrace the cyclical reality of winter rather than seek to avoid it. We are powerless against the magisterial forces of winter—but we can control our response.

So let's light some candles. Let's cut generous slices of this very moist cake. Here, take a cup of steaming tea and a woolen blanket, and let's sit together awhile by the fire.

*

But what happens when the fire dies and plates of cake sit empty and your friends say their goodbyes at the end of the night?

Brute winter forces everyone to face, not only their own vulnerability, but their own emptiness. How to fill the massive vacuum of wintertime? Often at night, my mind begins to drift down darkly as if weighted with the gravity of the set sun. Boredom looms. The TV is not enough. Books are not enough. Plated sweets are not enough. I begin to question myself, and everything I thought was good grays in old shadows. I am afraid. I snuff myself in sleep.

But perhaps this is part of the truth winter whispers: an invitation to listen to emptiness rather than scurry to fill it.

Writing out of the monastic cell's severe quiet, Kathleen Norris asks, "What would I find in my own heart if the noise of the world were silenced? Who would I be? Who will I be, when loss or crisis or the depredations of time take away the trappings of success, of self-importance, even personality itself?"[8]

These bare trees have something to teach me.

*

Winter challenges me to discipline my eyes to see, but also to trust there is much I do not see. I do not see the universe underneath the snow-lace, the narrow sheaths of ice that break brittle with a toe tap. I do not see the latent seeds resting in the womb of the earth, just as I do not see the child being formed inside my body. Growing things require darkness, long before light.

*

And, in my corner of the world, cold. A deep, acerbic cold. Temperatures must fall below freezing to kill insects and pathogens that prey on good, green things. The cold, then, is like a metamorphic cleansing.

As a young child, I would find warts bubbling on my fingers. My pediatrician's solution: killing them with cold. Liquid nitrogen can freeze warts away. I remember the procedure being painful and I never wanted to do it again. But eventually my warts dissolved.

What if I let the cold cleanse my own heart? What festering diseases must die? What will I lose if I refuse the chill, escape to palmed beaches in my mind? How might holy ice transform the bare and budless into a thriving canopy of green?

*

The cold can be so deep, it seems to kill everything good and green, along with the parasitic and destructive. But this snow slumber, too, is necessary. In dormancy, growth temporarily halts. Plants hold their energy in reserve for new growth, conserving themselves for the green burst of spring. During these "chilling hours," farmers can prune and transplant without harming the green beings that form their livelihood. Without enough chilling hours, the plant will produce fewer, weaker buds and will ultimately be less fruitful.

I am no farmer, only indirectly dependent on the shifting seasons. But the cold naturally hems me inside. I tend to sleep more, moving with the rhythms of the waning sun. As a teacher, I am grateful for a couple of weeks of dormancy between semesters. When the fields lie fallow, I have space to walk long walks, to pray unhurried prayers. Without this rest, I could not sustain my labors; I would have left teaching years ago.

*

No matter how useful winter is, biologically or otherwise, it can feel so very long. God could have created a winterless world, one where harvest gentled directly into spring. But instead God chose to embed many ecosystems with long stretches of barrenness and rest and cold. God intended winter as an essential caesura in the rhythm of life for much of earthkind.

God intended this space of futility, the absence of natural flutter and action. Bears slumber in hidden hollows. Humans shutter their doors and huddle under blankets. The farmer must pause, empty-handed. The world must wait for the cold to do its cleansing, for things once green to rest, for seeds to gestate in the earth: a metamorphosis unseen.

*

God has sung slumber into the orchestration of our spiritual life, just as our earthly one. The God who spoke the universe into being could have redeemed it with a word. But after the bitten fruit and shifted blame, God chose to lead humanity through a white desert of pause. Apt how Christmas falls in the wintertime, just after the darkest day of the year. Apt this call to hope even in the midst of what feels like endless waiting.

Christmas: the celebration of the arrival of the Messiah. So long, the wait. A wait that begins in the ruined Garden with a promise of redemption from a woman's seed. A seed that lies dormant in darkness for millennia. For millennia, God sings this promise through the prophets.

God hides hints in the stench of sacrifice and the way a lamb's blood painted over a door was a grace. But only hints, shadows. Generations upon generations would puzzle the hints, dream meanings into the words of breath. Generations would puzzle and hope and die, without ever seeing even the palest of seedlings crack the dust of the earth. Without ever understanding the mystery.

And then, silence. No recorded words from God for four hundred years between Malachi and Matthew. Four hundred years ago seems unfathomably far away: the waning of the Ming dynasty, the inception of the American slave trade. Four hundred years from now, I will be so long forgotten it will be as if I never breathed.

Imagine: this seeming eternity of silence.

Then—even when the Messiah arrives on the earth, he hides in the darkness of a womb. The size of an orchid seed, he must wait for nine months as the cells divide and redivide, form skin and heart and lung. And after the Messiah is born, the world must wait thirty years for the swaddled babe to grow into a boy and the boy into a man who will return to the dark and die.

*

And live again. Emerging from the hollow tomb, the Messiah awakens like all the splendor of spring bound in one body. Indeed, his rising is the only force that makes spring possible, makes hope possible at all.

*

But the Messiah awakens only after a wait of three days. Spring too soon is dangerous.

In false springs, awakened plants may produce essential petals quickly lost in a sudden hard freeze. Mild winters and harsh springs cost fruit growers billions of dollars. Prematurely warm temperatures affect wildlife as well. The pied flycatcher has experienced a severe population decline over the past two decades as their prey now peaks too early in the season. Better suffer the bitter winter than starve in a precocious spring.

*

Much of my life, I've loathed the waiting, clamored for God to move, to act. Enough of this dead winter. I want movement, spring. If my young-adult self could have ruled the world, I would have married much sooner (how long the weeping, lonely movie nights when I'd shovel sugar into my face with a spoon). I would have had a baby sooner (how long the months of trying, the sense of futility, the fear that something was, fundamentally, not right). We would have bought the first house we wanted, not the third (how despairing, in the throes of our middle-class entitlement, to lose what we felt was our dream house, twice).

Now I am grateful for those seasons of waiting. I am grateful I had more time in my twenties to travel, to become, to spend unhurried hours with God. I am grateful for the months of waiting to conceive, the months my husband and I bore the gift of anticipation, of kneeling in God's presence together again and again. I am grateful we didn't get the first house, or the second. The third was just right.

Some timings I do not understand. Some still frustrate me. I'm still waiting for some to be fulfilled. I am waiting for peace in my husband's home country of Ethiopia. I am waiting for the baby in my womb to breathe the same oxygen as me. I will always wait. Winter will always be a part of my life, the seasons braided in complicated harmonies.

*

Perhaps I can call winter good for the same reason a good story is good. The greatest stories are those that bravely pass through moments and seasons of the deepest of dark. The full weight of despair pushes our hero right to the tip of hopelessness. Before the burn of Mount Doom, Frodo refuses to destroy the ring and save Middle Earth. Charles Wallace gives in to the overwhelming pulse of It. The Messiah, the only, the so long-awaited hope, dies and is buried.

And yet, there is a yet.

Somehow, by a strange grace, the story continues. Mary Magdalene meets a breathing Messiah in the Sunday morning garden. The redemption is kaleidoscopically bright only because it comes after a long, long darkness. Winter. Perhaps this is why, after months of dark, white days, I feel such an unusual joy at the crocus, yellow and unsnowed.

Part Four:
Motherhood

laundry and liturgy:

on cleaning

What I do must be done
each day, in every season,
like liturgy. I pray

—Kathleen Norris, "Housecleaning"

A gain, this morning. Pressing the soap dispenser's head, honey-colored liquid easing onto a washcloth. Holding a blue bowl, a silver spoon, a tea-tinted mug, and thumbing the curves. Finger pressure seeking out shadows. Gripping a mussed scrub brush for the plates speckled in last night's dinner. And for the broiler pans, the stainless steel scouring pad like a woven coat of mail. Then, a gentle twist of the faucet handle, a sluice of warm water slipping over bowl, spoon, mug, plate, pan. Once sprinkled, each piece returns to its original colors. Warm as if quickened to life for a few seconds, they radiate the heat, the ebullience, of cleansing.

*

Just over six months ago, I gave birth to my firstborn son. Soon after, I decided to leave my nine-year teaching career to be, as the modern parlance has it, a "stay-at-home mom." My life now moves to new rhythms, ordered primarily by the cycles of my son's hours of waking, playing, and sleeping. And though I certainly cleaned before, my presence at home makes me more attuned to the cycles of cleanliness.

Scrubbing the toilet. Wiping the countertops. Vacuuming the carpets. Dishes. Laundry. (The dreaded) dusting. I am constantly cleaning something, from feet to floors. Sometimes the labor seems meaningless, because it never ends. The moment a cup is cleaned, someone is thirsty. The moment I brush a feather duster over the shelved trinkets, a new layer of star dust and dust mites, soil and cells, again descends.

*

More than any housewife, God cares about clean. In the Old Testament, God names things Clean or Unclean, detailing scrupulous instructions for differentiating between the two. Unclean: carcasses, cadavers, mold, disease, blood, flying insects, swarming animals, menstrual blood, semen, animals that do not chew cud or lack a cloven hoof, sea creatures without fins and scales, birds who eat what is already dead. Clean: just about everything else. Like an OCD parent, God demands anyone or anything that has even the slightest contact with the unclean to be scoured and scrubbed, and even in some cases, destroyed.

Without washing, intimate communion with God is impossible.

Before God descends from Mount Sinai, the Israelites must launder their clothes.[1] The unclean must sprinkle themselves in pure water, in minty hyssop.[2] Before entering the sanctuary, Levites must wash their hands and feet in a laver of bronze.[3] In the Apocalypse, the great multitude of saints who worship in the throne room must bleach their clothes in the blood of the Lamb.[4]

I imagine for desert-dwellers, the imperative to wash with water carried weight. How careful the ancient Israelites must have been to avoid a wayside carcass or the spray of blood from a sacrificed lamb knowing the effort required to find water and wash. What if no water could be found? Did the rhythms of life cease and an itchy, isolated in-between begin until an oasis could be found? Did the unclean hunger for the sanctuary, for God?

*

I am trying to understand what the Benedictines mean when they say *ora et labora*. Why for hundreds of years these communities have structured their lives around hours dedicated to both prayer, and work. Robed in T-shirt and cut-off jeans, I kneel on the linoleum. It is the chore hour, after the hour of *lectio*, before the hour of communion with the notably chubby six-month-old novitiate. I press a damp cloth over each square, back-and-forth-and-back. Back-and-forth-and-back I erase shoe scuff and dried clots of tomato juice. With the back-and-forth-and-back of my hands, I loosen the fetters of my mind.

New-opened, I try to listen.

Slipping out of the Psalms and into scrubbing allows me to ponder while I work. I work out written truths through my body. My body becomes a breathing sacrifice, pouring energy onto floors so my beloveds can walk over them in peace.

Other times, I make lists of things I am grateful for: *Thank you for the grace of breath. Thank you for the cup of orchid tea. Thank you for my son's look of wonder as I dab peanut butter onto his tongue.* And lists of needs: *have mercy on Ethiopia, heal my friend with cancer, strengthen me after another sleepless night.*

Here on this hallowed linoleum ground, I pray.

The lists, like the chores, are endless. But also endless are the moments to receive God's mercies, daily grace. Through prayer, I can surrender the hours of labor for divine transformation into something life-giving, creative, holy.

*

How delightful the expression "cake of soap." It dubs a banal ritual, washing the body, with a celebratory shimmer. Standing before the sink, I grasp the little white cake of soap. Cake of soap. I roll the slippery square between my palms, return the cake to its fitted ledge. My hands cup against each other, taking turns holding fists. They flatten palm to palm, fingertips slightly bowed, as if in gleeful expectation or prayer, before clasping together like lovers' hands. My hands dance these steps again, again. Clear water slides the soap away and I press my damp hands in a towel. Cleansed, my hands are ready to hold a baby or dice onions or eat a sandwich or mop a floor. Cake of soap.

*

Labor can be holy, but it can just as easily shift profane. Sometimes I take the stuff of labor and deform it into complaint, each stroke of the washcloth stoking bitterness. Or I disfigure sweeping and dusting into reasons for my worth. Polishing figurines to polish my own ego. I want those who enter my home to know, not the glorious love of God, but the glory of me.

O God, forgive my dark ingratitude, my bitter heart. May my labors root and blossom in love.

*

Dish-washing and floor-wiping can be apt times for confession. For one, the posture seems fitting: my body is bent, either my neck (in washing) or my knees (in wiping). And I know my need to confess never ends, like the opportunities for cleaning. From the moment I awaken, my soul gathers grit. Even before shifting vertical from my sheets: *I demand more sleep. I can't do everything I must do today. I will not make the effort to say good morning to my husband before he leaves.* And those are just the dusty bits I notice.

But each confession unclouds a little more of my dusty soul. Lets in a little more light. As I wash the plastic bags to be reused again, I know I will find the sweet of forgiveness again. And again.

*

After hours of laboring, after the obstetrician cut a six-inch slit in my body and guided a baby out, after my skin was sewn shut, after a day and night of colostrum dribbling from my breasts, the doctor told me I had one job to do: take a shower. I remember shuffling to the bathroom, feeling as if my insides would at any moment tumble from the raw incision. I remember taking ginger steps through the opened glass door and shifting on the tap. I remember the ribbons of warm water gliding down my temples, my spine. I remember washing away the dried milk and blood and sweat, then peeling back the gauze and tape, still too scared and bloated to look at my scar. I remember emerging from the shower, new-rinsed. Glorious, luminous, this feeling of cleansing.

*

As a COVID survivor and former teacher, I wash my hands often. Carefully attuned to the invisible reality of noxious microorganisms crawling about, I wash after weeding the garden and before dinner and following the multitudinous errands that stretch in between. Cleanliness, the kind that protects from disease and safeguards health, requires vigilance.

Like invisible pathogens, evil also germs on a plane I cannot see. In Psalm 119 the poet prays, *How can a young man keep his way pure? / By guarding it according to your word.* The word "guarding" comes from the Hebrew *šāmar*, which can mean "to attend to, beware, be circumspect, keep, watch." Here is a call to attend to the cleansing of my inner being, as watchfully as I do to my body. To guard my soul from evil germing as I would a newborn from infectious bacteria.

My son was born in pandemic confinement. Before his birth, my husband ordered a fresh box of masks and even a package of face shields. We strategized as to which visitors could hold our son and how many we could safely allow in our living room— that is, if we allowed any at all. As I was just recovering from COVID myself, my husband and I were sequestered in a quarantined hospital room. Some nurses entered in hazmat suits, and with each entry and exit, all of them pressed foamy sanitizer onto their palms. No visitors could enter the hospital, not even my mother. (And without a negative COVID test, even my husband would've been denied entry.) Driving home from the hospital, my husband bought a gallon-size jug of off-brand Purell.

The word "pure" in Psalm 119 comes from the Hebrew *zākâ*, figuratively meaning "to be innocent or clean" but literally "to be translucent." Not clear enough to reveal every daily detail, only what is most important: light. What if I attended to my soul as many times as I washed my hands each day? If I brought my heart to the basin with my hands, opening myself to mull the Word, to listen, to confess? If I tended my soul like a newborn babe? Divine light might have more of a chance to filter through to those around me, like Sunday morning sunshine through stained glass.

*

After sprinkling the tub with Comet, after bending into the basin (rather awkwardly, rear end up) to scrub away the shadows left after bathing, I imagine my home as a kind of sanctuary. I imagine the window glass infused with colored stain and stories. I imagine the porch a kind of airy narthex, the living room with its couches and chair, a nave. *How lovely is your dwelling place, O LORD of Hosts!* I pray.[5]

During the pandemic lockdown, my husband and I entered church through a screen. For the Eucharist, my husband would pour Vimto mixed with water into tiny porcelain cups, then sever and serve bits of bread. Seated on the couch cushions before the blue light of the television, we would consume the Host.

In the dining room I imagine as a refectory, I whisk coils of lost hair and brittle bits of leaves into a dustpan. I am preparing the sanctuary, sweeping hardwood like it was holy ground. Cleaning up for angels dressed as strangers. Or (more likely) for saints garbed in jeans. Or—I dearly hope—for an encounter with God.

*

Until recently I thought God's heightened attention to detail in the levitical law seemed rather anal—evidence of a judgmental, nitpicky God. But in *The Quotidian Mysteries*, Kathleen Norris suggests this care for human minutiae reveals divine love. In fixing his attention on the little things—how we cook, how we clean, how we live our domestic lives—God offers us the opportunity to involve him in all the crooks and crevices of our daily existence.

Hundreds of years after God gave Moses the divine cleaning checklists in the book of Leviticus, Emmanuel enters finity to be present: God with us. He slips into human skin, into human vestments that get dusty and dirty and in need of a thorough washing. He eats off dishes that must be scrubbed, with hands prone to grease and grime. As Norris writes, this is "a God who cares so much as to desire to be present to us in everything we do."[6]

*

Breathing moist air, I kneel against the bathroom tile, rest my elbows on the tub's white rim. Holding the warm washcloth, I wipe the inner shadows of my son's baby ears, notice the gentle architecture of helix, cavum, lobe. The sudsy cloth follows the contours of scapula and spine, collar bone and belly. Each toe, each finger. Every hollow and crevice.

Washing becomes attention becomes prayer. And I see my son as if for the first time.

Washing ankle and knuckle reminds me how the body, like the home, can be a temple. God dwells here, amidst the damp towels and tepid water. God dwells in this frame of tissue of bone.

God dwells here.

*

Like an artist, one who cleans well becomes intimately acquainted with the details of an object—and believes such details are worthy of attention.

Perhaps it is because I don't often clean like an artist that I find dusting so dreadful.

Take the bookshelves, for instance: the crystal vase too fine for flowers. (*Waterford Crystal*, my late Nana said as she handed it to me.) A tiny carved box that carried our wedding rings down the aisle. An emptied cassette holder displaying bills and coins from my husband's country, the one he left. A glass jar from which (according to a note in my late Grandpa's hand) I ate my first bite of banana. When I brush the feathers over each relic, I remember: You clean what you care for. Only the dispensable, the rubbish-bound, does not merit the gift of cleansing.

It's like this: imagine you are a piece of glasswork burned, inspirited, and poised in a gallery. Imagine waiting on a shelf for a day, for a century. Each moment, fairylike iotas of dust gather over your arms. Imagine yourself graying with each layer of abandon. Then, like Ezekiel prophesies: God cradles you, the castoff, in his hands.[7] God gathers you so close to his breast you can feel his heartbeat. Gentle, God empties you of everything unclean. God lays you under a silver spigot and washes you in warm water, in the blood from his own body, until you are the color you were meant to always be.

Because you were not made for destruction, but love.

*

When I was growing up, my mom would say that God is a God of order, particularly when the house needed cleaning. Take creation: God creating a world from void. Ordering night and day, sea and sky. Ordering six days of labor, and one for rest. *Kosmos*, a Greek word often translated as "world," can literally mean "something ordered."[8]

One could even say that Jesus was birthed onto human soil to clean, washing the defiled of their death and disease, becoming the ultimate cleansing for humans who could not cleanse themselves. Jesus touches the Unclean: lepers, a bleeding woman, dead and diseased bodies. Rather than be soiled, this God with skin purifies these dusty souls, scrubbing them whole so they can once again curl up on the divine bosom.

Like a feverish housewife attacking a filthy floor with a broom, Jesus scours the temple of dirty money and money lenders. He guards the purity of his Father's house with zealous attention. And the book of John suggests that Jesus was the type that made his bed each morning.⁹ Upon waking from death, one of Jesus's first actions is to tidy his berth, neatly folding his face covering before leaving the tomb and altering reality for all time.

Those who clean cabinets and coats and cups image their divine nature as they scrub. Cleaning is a way of setting things right in a universe that tends, by natural law, to disorder. In their own small way, the wielders of brooms and mops are fighting for whole and good things: clarity, order, peace. Laboring to hold back chaos.

*

Each headline falls like a weight, one after another, after another: *Ukraine falls. Earthquake batters Haiti. Hurricane Grace drowns Mexico.* I want to help somehow. But the pitiful checks I send to charities seem pointless, my prayer soundless.

And yet. There's something about cleaning that gives hope. Living creates spaces of disorder: a speckled mirror, a limescale-encrusted kettle, a counter crammed with dishes piled into each other like nesting dolls. Each exists as a problem of sorts. But in a short space of time, even fifteen minutes, I can wipe a mirror and scrub out a kettle. I can solve a problem. This is no small thing. Norris: "There are days when it seems a miracle to be able to make dirty things clean."¹⁰

Even though making dirty things clean does not directly touch those in need, the act reminds me I am not powerless. It helps me to focus on what I can change. I cannot fight the Taliban or free the Uighurs. I cannot heal my dying friend of cancer. But I can try to order my own tiny square of earth. I can wash a sink-load of dishes.

*

God bless the janitors. God bless the garbage workers. God bless the maids. God bless the window washers, dangling from threads above city streets. God bless the invisible, forgotten hands that make mirrors shine again after the lights go out in fluorescent-lit schools, churches, skyscrapers. God bless those who have laundered soiled bed sheets three mornings this week already. God bless those who wipe goopy noses and oatmeal-smeared faces. God bless those who dust the top shelf nobody sees. God bless you, Keepers of Order, Renewers of Things, for Jesus said the meek will inherit the earth.

*

The night Jesus is betrayed, his disciples are gathered around platters of warm bread, aromatic lamb, new-culled olives and dates. They gulp draughts of wine in between bites. Perhaps Peter is telling another story. While everyone else is still guzzling wine and popping olives into their mouths, Jesus leaves his place at the table, takes off his outer garments, and wraps a towel around his waist. He pours water into a nearby basin and kneels before each disciple. He unties the knots in each sweaty sandal, gingerly slipping out bare feet. With gentle reverence, he holds each naked heel in his palm, as if touching temples. He does not make a face at the stench, the sight of crusted manure in between toes, toenails black with dust.

Like a mother, he cradles these feet fuming with everywhere and everyone they've encountered. With uncanny tenderness, his fingers massage away the dead skin and grit. Then he lifts each newly-baptized foot from the basin, and dries it with a towel in his lap.[11]

At the end, Jesus tells his disciples to do likewise. Jesus tells us to do likewise. To be the kind of people who wash stinky feet, who rinse away mire, who are not afraid of dust and dirt. Who participate in communal cleansing, ritual renewings. Again and again.

*

Perhaps the pandemic has revealed more than any other time in recent human history how washing hands is a way of serving one's neighbor. Keeping clean is a way of protecting the vulnerable—the elderly, the mother-with-child, the immuno-compromised—so close to Jesus's heart.

And it's not just my body I am called to keep clean for the sake of my sister and brother. All of my sins (even the most secret) influence those around me and by extension the workings of the whole earthly community. I share a portion of the responsibility for the crimes committed in my neighborhood and beyond.

When I shout at my son, I contribute to a culture of impatience and aggression. When I pretend not to see the woman with a cardboard sign standing on a concrete median, I refuse to allow God to be present to her through a toothbrush or a bag of muffins. When I ignore divine nudges to care for my community—ladle soup, pick up litter, vote—I am Cain shirking the burden of brotherhood.

These are things I cannot wash my hands of.

But in the same way, all of the good, creative acts God does through me ripple through the universe in ways I cannot fully see. When I allow God into the minutiae of daily life, divine power circulates through everything I do: from scrubbing floors in prayer to bathing my son in reverence. In cleaning, as in any kind of labor, I become a co-creator.[12] Tending to my own heart is a way of tending to the heart of the world.

Cleaning then, can be a way of love.

*

Love is this: Jesus, the holy God-Man, not only seeks out the Unclean (dirty feet and dusty souls), not only touches the leprous and foul. He becomes, in St. Paul's words, sin.[13] God becomes Unclean. And, as divine law demands, the Unclean must be destroyed. On the skull-shaped hill, Jesus's body reeks of sweat and blood and soon stiffens into a corpse.

It is only after days dead in a tomb, that Jesus rises as he rose from the Jordan waters, wet and woken as a newborn.

If God so loved the world, how can I shirk the nicotine-stained hands of the man holding a styrofoam cup on the sidewalk? How can I call scouring blackened pots unworthy work? When faced with muddy toes and grimy glasses, how can I do anything but rejoice in the opportunity to embody Jesus, believing that in plunging myself breathless beneath the waters of self-loss, I will be born again?

*

Brother Lawrence, who served as a lowly cook in a Parisian monastery, wrote that "we can do little things for God; I turn the cake that is frying on the pan for love of him."[14][15]

This can be love: wiping dried spaghetti sauce from the inside of the microwave. Scraping scum from the toilet's hinges. Buffing scuffed shoes. Bleaching stained underwear. Renewing a mired pan to its original form. Collapsing cobwebs with broom handles. Washing grubby toddler feet. Offering bottles of water to people without homes. Holding the hands of the diseased and dying. Incarnating, in the folds of daily existence, the Great Cleanser, the God Who Purifies and Is Pure.

*

And yet. What if the laundry (inevitably) begins to mountain? What if the counters clog with stacked bowls and unopened mail and strawberry-stained shirts for days, weeks? My home will never, ever be completely, wholly clean. But I can take one step, take those small, Spirit-led steps each day. Guzzling grace all the while. And that is enough.

Until that day when the veil is torn in two, there will always be a spoon left in the sink.

*

I imagine my home as a haven. Windows clarified in confession. Floors swept open with thanksgiving. Green leaves unfurling from quiet pots like prayers. It is a space ready, expectant, to metamorphose into whatever it needs to become: a place of nourishment, hospitality, play. Walls scrubbed translucent, my home, alive with heartbeats, becomes an echo chamber of light.

*

Most Mondays, I wash the dishes piled up from a laborless Sunday. It daunts me the perils of encrusted bowls and burnt pans and cloudy silverware that seem to have mysteriously multiplied overnight. Taking a breath, I plunge into the foul, germy mess. Start with a spoon. Here, down in the daily dust and detritus—this dark matter strangely cleansing—I labor.

But after descending (again, again) like the diseased leaping into the womb-dark depths of Bethsaida's angel-stirred pool, I will rise (again, again) like one birthed from water: washed, that is, healed.

the wakeful desert:

on sleep deprivation

Lo Contemplation lifts th'attentive eye, / To view the splendor of the spangled sky.

—*Phillis Wheatley, "Night: A Poem"*

S leep deprivation is an emptiness expanding. Your mind, which used to tick along with such nimble precision, opens like a void, like someone spooned all the gray matter out. Memory and thought pass through like wispy clouds on a hard blue sky. You try to grasp them, but they flutter away or dissolve like fog in your fingers.

The problems of the day—what to eat for breakfast and when was the last time you showered and where your keys are—cycle through the deep space of your mind again and again but you can't quite figure out the answer. Or you pedal between two choices (oatmeal with banana or apple?) before landing on a completely different one (pancakes!).

Your body, too, echoes vacuous, wobbling as if its structural center has floated away, as if wrestling with Jupiter's hefty gravity. Or perhaps it's just your hollow head that throws the rest of your bones out of balance. Energy evaporates and your vacated muscles leave you falling into pillows and chairs and floors. You try to fill the void with quick sugar like candy, but in seconds it evaporates.

*

I've never been a good sleeper. Even as a child, I would rise in the dark, pad my bare feet to the living room aglow with lamps and laugh tracks, and complain to my parents that I could not sleep. My father is an old hand at insomnia and would suggest a glass of milk warmed in the microwave. The refrigerator bulb would capture my shadow opening the door, gripping the plastic gallon jug, pouring half a glass of two percent. I would drink the milk alone in the starlit kitchen.

Perhaps due to my childhood insomnia, I became greedy for sleep, hoarding hours like Hershey bars. I hated elementary school sleepovers, how the powdered donuts in the sharp morning light only intensified the hangover of sleeplessness. When a flock of cousins would spend the night with my three siblings and me, I would hole up in my bed at what I deemed a reasonable hour (which was earlier than even what my parents imposed). Of course it's impossible to expect flocks of cousins to be quiet, so I would groan at each squeal and giggle and mysterious thud that slipped through the feather pillows I'd stacked over my head. And eventually anger to the tip of explosion, wrathfully whipping the door open where they were corralled in joyous nighttime play.

During university I successfully avoided having to "pull an all-nighter," and when I taught in Ethiopia as a fresh graduate, I would be in bed most times by missionary midnight: nine p.m. Dubbed "grandma" by more owlish friends and family, I still leave parties early (dreading the New Year's ritual of staying up till the ball drops) and slip into the bedcovers, insatiable for sleep.

*

Motherhood has only whetted this insatiability. As of my firstborn's ninth month, I haven't slept a full eight hours in over a year and have been chronically sleep-deprived since his birth. I crave hours of sleep, piecing bits together here and there between nighttime feedings, trying to cobble up a few sweet minutes during the day (unsuccessfully)—and it's never quite enough.

Recently I've found my prided grammar breaking down, my speech reduced to a kind of pidgin, all infinitives and missing articles. When my husband recently asked me how to warm a pizza, all I could muster was, "Broil. Low. Five minutes." And yesterday for church, I dressed my son in pink socks and stained dragon sweatpants and a flannel plaid shirt that was too small. During book discussions it's all I can do to let ideas wash through my sieve of a brain, hoping for something to hold by the end. Forget about remembering anything unrelated to daily survival (the names of neighbors, the plots of novels). Mental math is a virtual impossibility. My favorite words now: "I don't know."

My father often tells me he listens to what difficult circumstances have to teach. More by example than by words, he gently offers this suggestion, as he would a glass of warm milk. When I listen to sleep lack, I begin to wonder if, after all my years of slumber-greed, God is lovingly leading me into a sleep desert. Away from the somniferous trove where I'd amassed honeyed hours of delicious oblivion. A trove that, though it disappeared each morning, provided me with the intellectual vim and emotional balance to sort through the day's problems, the physical stamina to juggle *choppingscrubbingchasingrunning*, the refreshment to begin each day with something like hope. Insomnia has long been one of my greatest fears. How to survive without sleep? And what is God whispering in these desert winds?

*

On our evening stroll, I explain to my husband how sleep deprivation feels like fasting. You're existing without a crucial, life-giving need being met. You're hungry all the time, but for rest rather than food. You're holding a gaping lack inside, a secret, invisible emptiness. And it pushes you, in the quandary of quotidian details, to look up: pray.

Sleep deprivation has long been tied to spiritual discipline. The desert mothers and fathers (third-to-seventh-century as-cetics[1] who sought God in Middle Eastern deserts[2]) strove to eradicate any element of their lives that hindered pure com-munion with God, including sleep.[3] Sleeping arrangements—a reed mat, a pile of straw, a single sheet of sheepskin—were in-tentionally disruptive to slumber. Many slept only sitting up or on a reclining seat to remain alert.[4] "One hour's sleep a night is enough for a monk if he is a fighter," said Abba Arsenius.[5] This same father (who deemed sleep a "wicked servant") would pass whole nights awake.[6] And Abba Bessarion testified, "For fourteen days and nights, I have stood upright in the midst of thorn-bushes, without sleeping."[7]

As one who sleeps on a thick mattress, padded in feather pillows, cool sheets, and a comforter, I find it difficult to sub-mit to such severity. I hold on to passages of Scripture like the one attributed to Solomon (divinely given *a wise and discerning mind* like none other[8]): *It is in vain that you rise up early / and go late to rest, / eating the bread of anxious toil; / for he gives to his beloved sleep.*[9] And David writes of his slumber, *I lay down and slept; / I woke again, for the LORD sustained me.*[10] Sleep is a gift from God, the fruit of humble trust in divine providence.

Even Jesus, who entered finity in a body, needed sleep. He repeatedly withdrew from the crowd to rest (which, I would assume, sometimes meant catching a few winks).[11] Once in a storm-tossed fishing boat, his shocked disciples found him sleeping on a pillow.[12]

The very creation God designed follows the ritual of cycli-cal oblivion. On the first day of world-making, God separated the light from the darkness, leading humans naturally into slumber with each set sun.[13] Whether nocturnal or otherwise, creatures rhythmically curl up in nests, caves, thickets, beds.

Perhaps many desert mothers and fathers would agree that sleep is a divine lullaby sung into the rhythm of creation. Indeed, they had to sleep at some point. But sleep deprivation as a spiritual practice? How could chronic sleeplessness be thought so essential for inner transformation?

*

In the first few months after my son was born, sleep lack shattered me. In between feedings, I was often too alert to sleep. As a fresh-born mother, I felt I had been baptized into a kind of feral awareness I'd never before experienced. At night I was obsessively attentive to my son's tiny exhales, his smallest whimpers. I was petrified he would stop breathing. Sometimes when I couldn't hear his breaths, I would stare at his chest until I saw the subtle rising. Meister Eckhart said "we are all meant to be mothers of God," and while his words are generally interpreted to mean the process of birthing Christ within us, I wonder if they could allude to attending him as well. Would this kind of attentiveness, that of a mother for her child, be the kind of divine-ward attention the desert fathers and mothers cultivated in the dark?

In one sense, wakefulness could betray a lack of trust. In the raw days of early motherhood, I chose to eat anxious bread rather than let God hold my son through the night. Just as I give my son milk when he wakes (as my father would offer it for my childhood insomnia), God offers the divine breast in the night when shadows glower. Holy eyes watch over my slumber like a mother over her newborn's. Could humility be the opposite of sleeplessness? But if wakefulness is rooted in trust and ferocious motherlove, if it attunes me to God's subtlest flutters, I wonder what gifts might bloom in the sunless hours. I wonder what I might see.

Though the desert mothers and fathers acknowledged the necessity of some sleep, too much became a barrier to vision.

Abba Poemen said, "Because of our need to eat and to sleep, we do not see the simple things."[14] I think of biblical prophets like Zechariah, whom an angel *wakened . . . as a man who is wakened out of his sleep* in order to see a fantastic vision of a forty-nine-lipped lamp aglow between a pair of olive trees.[15] If sleeplessness cultivates vision, I wonder what simple things I am seeing now that I couldn't have seen with more sleep. Am I more aware of divine graces hidden in the weave of daily existence? Does God manifest Godself in uncanny ways in the dark? I think of those nights in deserted Ohioan cornfields or Montanan forests, far from the light-polluted city I call home: how glorious the Milky Ways, those galaxies of stars!

But in between those bursts of heavenly light, how deep the dark. How many times have I nursed my son in the night, fearful of the shadows in the corners, and prayed against any evil lurking there! Perhaps recalling St. Paul (*For we do not wrestle against flesh and blood*),[16] the desert fathers and mothers kept awake to guard against the attacks of the devil.[17] They testify to bone-and-muscle wrestlings with demons but were also highly attuned to the inner, unseen ones. St. Evagrius and others wrote of demons and evil thoughts synonymously. This rings true: I've found that in the night the mental shadows of untruth and anxiety expand out of proportion, take on fangs and scowls. Midnight wakefulness could be a call not only to enjoy the stars, but to fight.

*

In the dark newborn hours, I began to attune myself to God's voice. I recalled my mother telling me that struggling to sleep could be a divine call to intercede on behalf of someone else. I could exchange sleeplessness for prayerfulness. She told stories like the one of the gospel-salted old lady who arose in the night to pray, and at that very hour across the world someone's need was miraculously met. Hungry to redeem the sleepless hours (and also have something to keep me awake while my son nursed), I began to pray. Nestled against my son in the quiet night, God brought me people to pray for, including myself.

Other times I would savor morsels of Scripture. (Some of the desert fathers recommended passing half the night in sleep, the other half imbibing the Psalms.) But there was a sweetness in the silence, too, just being with God, enjoying the milk of his presence in the dark. Who knows how secret nighttime prayers, the hidden words of healing and hope and anguish uttered by mothers in the Egyptian desert and in American cities, might nourish the catholic body of believers, and even the world?

*

According to the desert parents, the discipline of sleeplessness helped free them from their physical needs and desires, and ultimately, the imprisonment of their own wills. Abba Poemen, who often retreated for forty-day stretches, said, "I have discovered one simple thing: that if I say to my sleep, 'Go,' it goes, and if I say to it, 'Come,' it comes."[18] Sleeplessness is showing me that sleep is not my ultimate master, as fasting reminds me that I do not live by bread alone. Though sleep is as needful as physical sustenance, giving it up offers an opportunity to depend on preternatural grace. Sleep may be rooted in humility, but intentional, limited sleep deprivation (in the form of communal vigils or individual midnight prayers) could be too. In relinquishing sleep, the desert parents could entrust their vulnerable, wearied bodies and minds to the One who neither slumbers nor sleeps.

Sometimes, at its nadir, after weeks or months of little sleep, I feel a kind of exultation, a strange high. It's similar to a feeling I've felt during a fast, when I feel strangely liberated from the necessity of food and its time-consuming preparation. It's a heady feeling, the kind that comes while sipping a coupe of sparkling rosé on an empty stomach. Released from the gravity of sleep, I'm floating maybe, floating on a power beyond me.

In some desert (and European) monasteries, sleeplessness as a ritual became more elaborate. Medieval Benedictine monks went to bed at eight or nine p.m., then awoke for matins at midnight, lauds at three a.m., and prime at six a.m.[19] This rhythm could induce a state of chronic sleep deprivation, far from the doctor-recommended seven to nine hours. Modern monasteries seem to have less severe schedules. Saint John's Abbey in Collegeville, Minnesota, where Kathleen Norris lived while writing *The Cloister Walk*, bookends each day with prayers at seven in the morning and seven at night. Perhaps this shift in moderation is rooted in the reality that spiritual disciplines easily decompose into pride. Amma Syncletica said, "As long as we are in the monastery, obedience is preferable to asceticism. The one teaches pride, the other humility."[20]

Though harsh, the original monastic schedule holds some hope for a sleep-deprived mother like me. Like nursing mothers, these monks awoke at rhythmic intervals each night to feed each other (and themselves) prayers. Or perhaps it's more apt to say that, like babies, they awoke to be fed, God as mother alert to their tiniest whimpers. In the middle of the night when my son cries and I cannot sleep, I imagine God gently nudging my shoulders to receive a cup of sweet, nourishing milk.

*

In my husband's home country of Ethiopia, as in numerous faith communities around the world, vigils are embedded into the liturgical calendar. Though largely abandoned by many churches (including my own), this practice of communal nighttime prayer is not without scriptural basis. Just as David enjoyed the gift of sleep, he also gave it up to pray: *On my bed I remember you; I think of you through the watches of the night*[21] and *At midnight, I rise to praise you.*[22] Jesus calls his listeners to keep their lamps burning, remaining alert for his coming, *even if he comes in the middle of the night or toward daybreak.*[23] In the book of Acts, Sts. Paul and Silas pray and sing hymns *about midnight* from their prison cell.[24] I wonder, too, if the biblical prophets were woken in the deep space of night, St. John and Ezekiel chewing honeyed parchment in a kind of dream. What have churches missed in forgoing such midnight services? What have we lost in gaining sleep?

My husband has told me how the night before Easter and Christmas, believers attend church for prayer, fasting, and song. When I lived in Ethiopia, I would see the believers in the morning, as I drove to my own services. The worshippers would flock out of the church doors and gather along the road-sides, dressed in gauzy white *netelas* blinking in the sun. They would be walking to break their fast over tables laden with good things. My husband recalls those mornings of his child-hood, when the family would gather to feast on tender meats, lightly dressed greens, soft white cheese, a host of spiced stews—chickpea, lentil, potato, carrot, beet—and baskets of injera, crêpe-like bread rolled up in scrolls.

*

After months of particularly egregious sleep deprivation, I Googled some of its side effects. Physically, the toll can range from the mild (lack of energy and weight gain) to the severe (diabetes, hypertension, cardiovascular disease, and even de-creased life expectancy). Emotionally, sleep deprivation leads to stress, anxiety, irritability. But what has been perhaps hard-est for me (as one who has always thrived in academics and rel-ished dense philosophers) has been the mental deterioration: slower thinking, impoverished memory, poor or risky decision making, hallucinations.

Weeks after my son was born, my husband would wake in the night to my thrashing about in bed, digging through the sheets, crying, "Where's the baby? Where's the baby? Where's the baby?" Even more recently, he heard a thud in the night and found me on the hardwood floor, searching under the bed, crying my son's name.

My hallucinations are evidence more of a madwoman than a mystic, but I'm intrigued by a *Psychology Today* article connecting the desert, sleep deprivation, and mystical experiences.[25] Considering the desert fathers and mothers, the psychologist recounts how the isolation and severe conditions of the desert (in addition to the self-imposed privations of food, shelter, and sleep) lent themselves to mysticism. Sleep loss in particular reduces our capacity for higher-level critical thinking, thinking which may impede our ability to experience supernatural states of consciousness. Said another way: sleep loss could free us to apprehend the mystical. Modern psychology may use such science to explain away visions like St. Julian of Norwich's hazelnut or St. Theresa of Avila's castle. But I wonder at how God could speak to human beings in a particular way, in a stratum beyond metacognition. Perhaps Abba Poeman was right when he said that sleep inhibited our ability to see.[26]

Again and again, mystics from St. John of the Cross to Meister Eckhart invite their followers to release their rational thought in order to better experience and understand God. Though suspicious of visions, the author of *The Cloud of Unknowing* encourages readers to "bide in this darkness" beyond the reaches of their knowledge, because God cannot be understood with reason.[27] In fact, the author argues that everything—sensory experience, memory, knowledge of any kind—should be "hid under a cloud of forgetting."[28] Surely the God who wired human brains reveals Godself in mind and memory, but to a sleep-deprived soul who cannot be trusted to remember much of anything, the possibility of experiencing God despite (and even through) brain fog is encouraging. Maybe in my fogginess, I have an opportunity to sense God in a different way than if I was fully rested. A heartening thought: God graciously and uniquely speaks to each of us, in whatever state we happen to be.

My son and I take daily walks, and on my sleepiest walks I simply exist. I am in a state of unthinking (because I cannot think). Sister Mary Margaret Funk, former prioress of a Benedictine monastery in my hometown, explains this experience: "I let my thoughts come and then let them go. When I do this, ceaseless prayer begins to rise . . . My mind is alert, awake, receiving."[29] Unthinking, I cannot form coherent thoughts, meal plan, arrange my schedule. Paradoxically, my sleepy mind can be more attentive, because I simply am. Unable to create, I can only hold out my hands to receive the gifts of creation. Senses abloom, I gawk at the autumnal light glowing in yellow leaves, a dying red bush rustling in a kind of flame. I am able to listen: to leaf chatter, to the creaks in my own body, to God. Maybe God has deprived me of sleep to pause my ceaseless stream of thoughts. To call me to quiet.

When I'm sleep-deprived, the controlled, prescriptive, selfish prayers I often pray on my walks dissolve. I cannot ask for specifics. Much of all I can muster is "God have mercy." *God have mercy on my mother. God have mercy on my father. God have mercy on my son.* Or (inspired by a scene of Fred Rogers praying at his bedside in *A Beautiful Day in the Neighborhood*), I simply say people's names. *Elaine, Don, Kaki, Papus, Dagi, Jeremiah* . . . All I can do is uphold each soul to God, allowing him to pray, to sustain my friends and family in the particular ways I cannot articulate. In this way I am, as Henri Nouwen suggests, bringing them into the presence of God, into God's heart.[30] And when even names elude me, I can fling groans heavenward.

*

In the midnight vigils, in the nighttime psalmody, in giving up not just sleep but food and home and family and every delicious taste of the world, the ultimate yearning of the desert mothers and fathers was simple: God. I'm reminded of Kierkegaard's definition of faith in *Fear and Trembling*: releasing something in obedience to God, and fully believing you will receive it back again.[31] To choose to release sleep, then, seems to be a kind of faith.

There is space to enact faith, too, when sleep is taken rather than given. (I can trust God's strength, that daily manna dewing in the wilderness, will uphold my weakened body.) But what if this sleep desert of early motherhood was preparation to practice, of my own volition, in my own small way, the spiritual discipline of sleeplessness?

On the night he was betrayed, hours before offering his own body to be broken on a tree, hours before shouldering the guilt of the ages—and the wrath of God—Jesus invites his disciples to pray with him. He returns, twice, to find them dozing. (I imagine myself crumpled in a heap of robes among them.) While Jesus was preparing to drink his bitter cup, he was offering a sweet one to his disciples: the milk of divine presence, of communion with God himself. Oh, that when God offers me the cup of prayer, I would drink it.

*

While discussing sleep deprivation the other day, a fellow weary mother and I lamented the challenges of our little ones' four a.m. wake-up calls. But then she reminded me about one of our former colleagues, an Ethiopian named Ruth. Ruth would often wake up at four in the morning, robes uncrumpled, and, of her own volition, pray. All my midnight prayer sessions have been unplanned, reactive. (I am awake because my son wakes. I am awake because, however much I want to, I cannot sleep.) I marvel at Ruth.

"That's where she found her joy," my friend said.

Joy. Not duty, not obligation. Joy. I wonder at this delight, not in hoarding hours of sleep like candy—but, like the desert mothers and fathers, in giving them up (*blessed are the hungry*) to feast on something richer, fuller (*for they shall be filled*): sweet scrolls unfurled, that dewy manna, *Logos* pressed to opened lips. And a cup, a breast, overflowing.

pinned thorax:

on pain

[The afflicted one] quivers like a butterfly pinned alive to a tray.

—*Simone Weil,* The Love of God and Affliction

Pain is a treasure, for it contains mercies.

—*Rumi, "Pain"*

My husband and I are driving to the airport to say goodbye to my sister and baby nephew. August morning heat blow-dries through slits of open window as he talks about his most recent basketball injuries, those lingering aches, those muscles that twist and jam on the court. Every Thursday morning, he wakes up at five a.m. to shoot hoops with some men from church, despite regular injuries: a bent and bloated pinkie that never did take its natural shape again, jammed thumbs, knees he's had to tape in place. Last year, after struggling with consistent back and shoulder pain, he spent six months and a wad of cash on a white-toothed, chesty-voiced chiropractor we fondly called one of "our quacks" (the other being my doctor, who is not a doctor at all). The pain, though somewhat lessened, remains. Perhaps my husband is pressing the tender places on his shoulder. Here, here, is where it hurts. "Without pain," he says, "we wouldn't know what's wrong."

*

"Where does it hurt?" my mother, my father, a teacher would ask when I howled after a fall. I would point. Here. There. Can't you see my grass-yellowed knees, dirt mixed with new slits in my skin?

Gentle hands would dab a warm washcloth over the skinned knee, washing the wound of earth and its impurities. Then a warning before the splash of hydrogen peroxide, the calming smear of antibacterial ointment. And of course the all-comforting Band-Aid. The scraped knee showed me I was loved.

I imagine my mother here, now, as we drive to the airport. I imagine my body small and childlike again, scooped into the fortressing curve of her arms.

"Where does it hurt?" she asks, intent as if my answer is the key to her universe. I touch my chest, my tummy. I spread my fingers because it hurts all around here; there is not one point of pain I can localize, the way my dad did when I was nine years old and Grandpa had just died and he pointed to his heart saying, "It hurts right here."

"What's wrong?" my mother asks. I ponder the imminent goodbyes. Is it the fear of change? How parting destabilizes and disorients? The reality of a life of limits, where nothing truly lasts?

I hope the pain is clarifying what is wrong, but also what is right: I mourn because I love and this means the pain is good.

*

Good: the pain, the sorrow, those "negative emotions," clarifying not only what is right, but what is important. I recall past partings, like the day I flew off to my first teaching job in Addis Ababa, Ethiopia. The embrace of each family member—mother, father, sister, sister, sister, brother—felt like a small death. That circle of huddled souls was all my world. My dad pointed to his heart (the same place he touched when his father died), "You have everything you need right here."

What is important now (on the ride to the airport): your sister and her son. What is not: the dress she borrowed and forgot to give back, the past you regret, your need to arrange everyone's lives like rows of glasses on a shelf.

*

In childhood, accidents felt routine: inevitable the scraped knees, bruised shins, scabby bare feet of children. Falling felt often. Falling from bikes, little half-blown balloons tied by the wheel to create a puttering sound, as if we were driving cars like grownups. Falling from the trees where I read novel after novel. Falling while running, running amidst the freedom of objectiveless chase. As an adult, it is rare to experience the sudden, blunt, visible pain of arrested play. I am a stranger to good old bloodied knees.

Is it fear that keeps me from tree-climbing, from running out of sheer joy? Is it fear that confines me to a cushioned existence in climate-controlled spaces with rehearsed safety protocols?

A peacetime child born into a safe and well-stocked bungalow, I sometimes believe it is possible to live a life without pain, a fantastical life of picket fences and weedless lawns, benumbed by ceaseless entertainment and packages that alight on the porch within hours of purchase. And I protest when this illusory machinery jams, as if pain were an alien injustice, a disruption of the havens I labor to create.

I have this illusion that I can control my steps, wise as I am to avoid the folly of bare feet. As a child whose old scabs had barely begun to heal before new ones formed, perhaps I unconsciously knew that pain was not a stray, random smack, but rather a primary color of human existence.

*

Despite my fear of pain or any shade of discomfort, I still choose to bear it sometimes. Sometimes, I don't take ibuprofen when menstrual cramps contract those tender places. Sometimes, I walk to the library when driving would be easier. Sometimes, I call when a text would avoid an unwanted conversation. Most times, I savor the aches after a long run. Maybe I'm afraid of comfort's lullaby, hushing, rendering me vulnerable to life's next tragedy and oblivious to the ones that exist everywhere always now.

I want to be ready, lamp lit.

*

"We need pain to survive," my husband continues, fingers slipping over the steering wheel as the highway rushes past. He is speaking purely in physical terms, his aching body testifying. As a teacher, I studied the brain's role in learning. How the amygdala (or lizard brain, as I would say to my freshmen) warns of danger. Here, reactions fire without thought: fight or flight. We choke on smoke and run from a burning room. We jump and cry when the pan handle's hot.

Pain guardrails us for our protection.

Not feeling pain can be dangerous. Diabetic patients lose blackened toes, feet, limbs, oblivious to infected wounds they cannot see. Addicted souls stupefy themselves with narcotics, which mask the sharp, red spark of reality. (Much like numbing comfort, the couches and chocolates and novels that entrap the moment they become ultimate.) Some of the youth I taught would slice their thighs and arms just to feel.

We pass green exit signs. The airport approaches closer, closer. Closer, the moment I am dreading. My sister and her son are moving, permanently as anything on this earth can be. My sister's name is Grace.

*

If we need physical pain to survive, do we also need emotional or psychological or mental pain in a similar way? (Do I need this body all in butterflies? This gut-trembling dread of letting go?) When, as novelist Julia Alvarez expresses it, "the peaks in that graph of normalcy" spike—the weddings and births, deaths and partings—my emotions remind me I am alive.[1] Alive to those sudden, inexorable forces of internal electricity shouting that I feel and therefore have being.

The butterflies inside quake with life.

*

My dad, whose graph of normalcy regularly peaks with migraines, tells me pain—that aggressive grace—is a teacher. Kahlil Gibran agrees: "Your pain is the breaking of the shell that encloses your understanding."[2] Pain can push me to pause and, if I let it, to reflect and learn.

Last year, chest pains warned me something was wrong, rang alarms in my amygdala. I'd felt them before—in the crush before the school day, in the whirl of burning garlic and blinking messages and a whimpering baby—but I finally started to listen to what Pain was saying, or rather to what God was saying through Pain.

And with her characteristic bluntness, Pain said, *Rest*.

For a couple of months, I quit writing blogs and articles and essays, sat in uncomfortable silence, listened to God. I started asking questions: *Why do I feel the pressure to rush (in everything, all the time)? Why the need for hyperproductivity? Why do I resist rest?* After a season of prayerful pause, I started, slowly, to write what I was hearing.

My life began to change, slowly, as oceans sculpt pebbles. Though ever seeking elusive balance, I started learning to hold my son on my lap after slipping on his dinosaur boots, just to enjoy his presence. To let the strewn toys lie and receive my husband's gaze when he tells me about his day. To ask for help.

Pain can be a healer.

*

Did pain exist before the bitten fruit in the first garden? Poisonous soursop seeds or rhubarb leaves did not exist. Feral fangs did not await flesh. Imagine a world of perfect weather, without danger of frostbite or sunburn. No lack. Imagine bodies functioning without flaw, without the hell of physical decay: headaches, diseases, cancers. Imagine weariness as an unknown sensation, work only sweet. Imagine a universe without mental or emotional or psychological trauma in that dwelling place of the divine: eternal, God-breathed beings not knowing how to wound each other, not needing to say goodbye.

Did routine accidents, falls over slippery surfaces, thumbjams exist? Maybe holy hands protected in these cases, where pain does now. Maybe after the fall, this divine intervention was replaced with pain.

Or, divine intervention took on a bitter shape.

*

Pain can be a cloaked grace. A harsh tonic. A masked embodiment of divine love.[3] Was it divine love that slipped into the cloak of chest pains and gripped me by the shoulders and sat me down in a kitchen chair and said, *Breathe*? Is it divine love that wears the pain of parting (arms hollowed out, vacant spaces at the table)?

*

What is certain: Divine love slipped into human skin. Love-Cloaked-as-Christ knew pain. He knew the pain of pressing through Mary's birth canal, knew the intimacy of Mary's encircling arms as she cleansed his scraped little-boy knees. A carpenter, he likely suffered cut fingers and overworked muscles. Love-Cloaked-as-Christ asked an outcast woman to quench his thirst and resisted the devil's attempts to sate his hunger. On a social level, he was rejected and despised, homely, the kind of person people pretended they hadn't seen.[4] His neighbors tried to kill him. His chosen disciples didn't understand him. And in the end, he submitted to flogging, crucifixion, and death. Parted even from his Father.

This cloaked Love fully understands the shaft of pain.

*

Pain impresses me like a knife blade to look up, to look beyond myself. So quick, so brutal, pain reminds me how fragile I am (it's ridiculous how little pain it takes to bend my knees, needy). For Simone Weil, the reality of our fragility is central to our very being—and one to receive with gratitude.

Blessedly, pain crushes our paper self-sufficiency. It opens us to receive Love's invitation to walk with him the holy way of suffering he sanctified in his bloodied body—and, as Weil suggests, the gift of being nailed with him at the very center of his cross.[5]

Here at the cruciform center we can embrace dying with Love, awaiting a very-soon quaking and the tomb cracked open in the Sunday morning garden.

*

Profoundly painful this pressing into the splintery wood with Christ, still and helpless as a pinned insect. Profoundly precise this pain, spearing the thorax's threadlike aorta.[6] Yet how profoundly intimate. Within a decade of losing his father, mother, and favorite brother, William Blake wrote, "Till our grief is fled an' gone / He doth sit by us and moan."[7] We are not called to dwell alone in suffering. The oppressed and afflicted and forsaken Christ sits and moans with us.

As Christ weeps with me, I am called to weep with the weeping. However ordinary the pain I have walked through, however small in the scope of universal human suffering, it is hollowing welcome spaces within me to hold the pain of others. On a day I cannot now see, will this trembly saying goodbye breathe open a sanctuary for those who know the pain of parting?

*

Pain can be a window to presence. Though we have to break the panes with a rock (hands splinter-torn), the window can open to a dark sky of stars.

One of my life's darkest skies was miscarriage. Less than two weeks after barely being able to speak for the joy of a positive pregnancy test, a clot the size of an unshelled egg fell splat on the bathroom floor. After my husband and I found each other's arms (trembling, quaking), he told my mother, who happened to be with us at the time. In her embrace, I became a little girl again with a bleeding knee I wasn't sure could ever be healed.

Just days before the anniversary of our miscarriage, a year later, I thought early blood was a sign of pregnancy, a sign that the last year's pain would be redeemed in new life. But the blood only increased, and I realized it was just an abnormal cycle. So exquisite, so precise, this pain: a needle pinning the thread of my aorta. Just so.

Pain nailed me to God.

But it took a journey to realize this.

Does God even see us? I asked my husband in the aftershocks of loss. *Does God even care?* And in my journal, I wrote, *You, Lord, have broken my heart.* In my secret heart, I wrestled with the voice of Job's bitter wife, *Curse God and die.*

Despite my doubt and anger, God cupped divine hands around me, as if I were a winged thing. God opened my eyes to his presence sitting and moaning at my bedside. Giving me the same story of calming the seas (*O ye of little faith!*) through a friend's text, through my Bible reading, through a nephew's

Bible storybook. Singing to my heart through an Amharic song my husband translated for me (*Does he see me when my days get dark? / When fear surrounds me? / When I lose hope and am utterly spent?/ Is my God close? / Yes, he sees, he will help me / His heart aches when I am in despair*). Just weeks later our Ethiopian pastor sang the same lyrics to the rhythm of his guitar and I fell knee-caps to the floor, face in the chair.

In Narnia, the mythic landscape of some of my favorite childhood novels, the Pevensies' disagreeable cousin Eustace has been transformed into a dragon to reflect the cruelty and greed of his own heart. Longing to be whole again, he tries to scrape off his armor of scales. But he is too weak. Aslan the lion offers to help. Recalling Aslan's nails tearing off his skin, Eustace says it was the worst pain he'd ever felt. "The very first tear he made was so deep that I thought it had gone right into my heart." (The impaling needle, the exquisite precision.) But once the painful metamorphosis is complete, he recounts:

> I was as smooth and soft as a peeled switch and smaller than I had been. Then he caught hold of me—I didn't like that much for I was very tender underneath now that I'd no skin on—and threw me into the water. It smarted like anything but only for a moment. After that it became perfectly delicious and as soon as I started swimming and splashing I found that all the pain had gone from my arm. And then I saw why. I'd turned into a boy again.[8]

Through the miscarriage and its aftermath, I became smaller and very tender. And, bit by bit, I became more human, that is, I began to metamorphose, slowly, more into a little Christ. I began to unlearn a posture of entitlement, ingratitude, and hardness of spirit. I began to relearn faith. Trusting in the mercy of a God whose mercies pain obscured.

Pain reveals the crusty scales of my heart. The idols, like control. It hurts, this process of watching my sister and nephew fly away. But maybe when I lean into pain, I am leaning into parts of myself that need metamorphosis. That need to die. Like Eustace, I must hold still in the divine embrace and let Love-Cloaked-as-Pain rip off the dragon scales.

*

Yet, how easy it is for me to see pain as an opaque barrier to happiness, rather than a translucent lens leading to God. An invitation to intimacy with Love. How quickly a headache can turn me inwards, blind, a mere body alit in pain. How quickly I allow pain to snuff God from my vision, refuse to let it do its tormenting, cleansing labor.

*

But if pain is a grace, it is also a curse. After the shifted blame in the Garden, pain became part of the divine punishment of creation. I felt this punishment, Eve's curse quaking, in laboring to birth my son two years before our miscarriage. During contractions, as I squeezed my husband's baseketball-bent fingers like a vise, I recalled a story a pregnant friend told me: Watching the agonized wrestling of a butterfly struggling from its sepulchral cocoon, an observer decided to ease the butterfly's pain and snipped the end of the cocoon to widen it. The butterfly indeed emerged with greater ease— but its wings hung useless. Without the struggle, the butterfly could not fly.

Without the pain, the butterfly would die.

Maybe some women would think me crazy (my mother included), but when I got the epidural, I felt a sense of loss, as if I was missing the fullest dimension of the experience of birth. Benumbed with narcotics, I could not feel my body wresting out a baby. Maybe choosing to bear pain (the long runs, the jammed thumbs) keeps us alert to danger. Maybe also it's like this: reaching the panorama at the mountaintop is all the more joyous and rich for the burning muscles required to reach it. Somehow, in a dimension I cannot see, there is a quickening purpose in pain.

Or: Perhaps I can only trust that God can take the stuff of pain, redeem it.

*

Sometimes, the stars are hard to see. Sometimes, I cannot hear what pain is saying for all its red, splotchy bleating and howls. I hunger for pain to have a clear reason. But trite comforts only mask the reality of suffering. Theologian David Bentley Hart argues the impossibility of assigning objective meaning to disasters like the 2004 tsunami that killed over 200,000 human beings in fourteen countries off the Indian Ocean.[9] We cannot, Hart says, explain away the destruction as a display of God's glory or judgment for sin. He recalls *The Brothers Karamazov*, when tortured, tender-hearted Ivan states that the good of all humanity is not worth even one child's suffering. The weights and balances of good and evil are not neat, here, now.

Evil forces still fly, chaotically, in this universe.

I ponder the over 50,000 human beings dead from the Israel-Palestine conflict. The hundreds of thousands more whose lives intersected with theirs, whose lives now gape with absence. The millions of Uyghurs suffocating in Chinese concentration camps. How bone-frail my friend felt in my desperate hug as we stood next to the casket of her husband.

Sometimes, I can't explain it.

*

Pain tells me the world is not what it was meant to be. Makes me restless, unsatisfied. It shakes me out of my illusion that I can build a heaven on earth. Perhaps a way forward is to accept that pain is sewn into the fabric of fallen human existence, and to apprehend the everyday graces we have as the true anomalies. I wonder what would happen if I adjusted my expectation of life altogether. Accepted my fragile frame of dust, gave thanks for the grace of weakness, which presses me into intimacy with Love. Expected pain, not fatalistically or cynically, but bravely, knowing God moves in pain, redeeming.

What if everyday graces—waking up breathing, inhaling the scent of earth after rain, spooning a nourishing bowl of homemade soup—were seen as unusual delights, as the unmerited favors they are?

*

The moment skids still for a second.

My husband and I have gathered with my mom, dad, and younger sisters in the airport rotunda, ceiling high and echoey. We stand before the terminal's entrance funneling rushing passengers through security and away. An unusual sense of levity surprises me. Each of us hugs Grace and her one-year-old goodbye. We each try to squeeze all our love into our biceps and forearms as we embrace, and we also whisper of our love, once more, just to make sure it's heard.

After losing sight of Grace in the meandering, dark queue, we stand lingering, suddenly more empty. We are unsure of the next step. "So, want to go out for lunch?" my mom suggests. Somehow, the thought of curving around a laden table, together, now and here, sounds right. A weight lifts somewhere over my sternum, strangely: that fine splintery shaft metamorphosed into light.

discussion guide

Would you like to discuss this book with friends, a book club, or a small group at church? Or, would you like to reflect further on the ideas in this book? Scan the QR code below to access the discussion guide for *In Praise of Houseflies*.

acknowledgments

The process of creating this book has taught me is that writing is a communal endeavor, deeply dependent on an awe-inspiring tapestry of interweavings seen and unseen: the great cloud of witnesses, the visible body of Christ, strangers and hidden angels—all held together by the One without whom we can do nothing.

Thank you to the editors who believed in the book's nascent heart early on: Father Michael Rennier who published a version of "A Long and Chilly Vigil: On Winter" on *Dappled Things*'s blog *Deep Down Things*; to Nathanael Lee Hansen who published a version of "The Wakeful Desert: On Sleep Deprivation" in *The Windhover* (Vol. 26.2); and to Julie Riddle who published a version of "Culled Salt: On Saying Goodbye" in *Rock & Sling* (Issue 16.1).

Thank you to Samantha Cabrera who warmly welcomed me to Calla Press and gave me a chance to share this book with the world. Thank you to Madison Aichele who gently, thoughtfully, and graciously guided me through the book publishing process. Thank you to Rosa Gilbert for her marketing assistance. Thank you to Lara D'Entremont, Kelly Flannery, Esther Gonzales, Meghan McDonagh, Karen Miller, and Allana Walker for your thoughtful edits.

Thank you to Seattle Pacific University's MFA community. Thank you to my mentors, Susanne Antonetta and Lauren F. Winner, as well as guiding forces Gregory Wolfe, Scott Cairns, and Robert Cording. Fellow graduates Callie Feyen and Amy Peterson offered helpful feedback on an essay that became the basis for this book, while Janay Garrick shaped another chapter, gave feedback on my book proposal, and offered faithful encouragement along the journey. Thank you also to Arthur Boers, Tessa Carman, Charlotte Donlon, Luke Taylor Gilstrap, Annelise Jolley, Catherine Ricketts, and Sarah L. Sanderson for your encouragement and guidance in the book-publishing process.

Thank you to the gifted writers in my writing group: fellow MFA graduates Carolyn Schulz-Rathbun, Patricia Peters, and Julie Lane-Gay. Your faithful and attentive readings and insightful feedback beautifully deepened the book. Your correspondence is a source not just of friendship, accountability, and writerly support, but of profound, Jesus-rich nourishment.

Thank you to the first brave readers who read the manuscript: Olivia Coons, J. Scott McElroy, Megan Nykamp, and Elaine Renollet. Your perspective and sacrificial offering of time were great gifts. Thank you also to One Fellowship Church, to those who graciously endorsed this book, and to the launch team for your kind support.

Thank you to the readers of my blog; your timely encouragement has given me just enough to keep going. A special thank you to Joy Ashbaugh for being faithfully present at every step of the process and, most of all, for upholding me weekly in prayer.

Thank you to my siblings Don, Grace, Gloria, Olivia, sister-in-love Jeanie, and brother-in-love Tim who have all cheered me on in the book-writing process, supporting not just my work but my soul. Thank you to my Ethiopian family, particularly Lakech, Girma, Michael, and Feven, for your immediate and heartfelt acceptance, faithful support, and joyous love.

Thank you for letting me share parts of your stories which are now interwoven with my own.

My parents, Donald and Elaine Renollet, laid the philosophical and spiritual foundation for this book. Your persistence in fighting the current of complaint and cynicism with gratitude and joy have shaped not only this book, but my very being. Thank you for your faithful encouragement of my writing and for lovingly letting me go in my pursuit of the financially questionable routes of creative writing and French at university, and then mission work in Ethiopia.

At many points along the journey of writing this book, I was close to giving up—but my patient, humble husband Dagi consistently, lovingly encouraged me to persevere. Thank you for your radical readiness to support, for speaking truth at the right moments, and for believing, not just in this book, but in the One who gives it breath. Thank you for the gift of your presence with me in this meandering journey, not just of book publishing, but of life. Thank you to my son Jeremiah. Your joyous presence has been an ineffable, lavish gift; how privileged I am to be your mama. May you grow up to embody the gratitude and joy modeled by your grandparents on both sides of the ocean.

Above all: thank you to God. All of my words, ideas, strength, breath, everything, everything—everything—originates in you and finds its ultimate end in you. May this offering bring you glory.

endnotes

introduction

1 Weil, Simone. "Contradiction" in *Gravity and Grace*. New York: Routledge, 1999. PDF.

2 Ecclesiastes 2:24 (KJV)

body laid bare: on humiliation

1 Weil, Simone. "Reflections on the Right Use of School Studies with a View to the Love of God" in *Waiting for God*. New York: Harper and Row, Publishers, 1973. PDF.

2 Glasscock, Lawan. "Living Fabric: Letitia Huckaby Talks to History." *Image*. No. 101 (2019).

secret ladder sanctum: on loneliness

1 Sesame Street. "Sesame Street–One of These Things (Is Not Like the Others) Lyrics." *SongLyrics*. December/18/2024. https://www.songlyrics.com/sesame-street/one-of-these-things-is-not-like-the-others-lyrics.

2 Lewis, C.S. "Let's Pretend" in *Mere Christianity*. New York: Harper One, 2001.

3 St. Teresa of Avila. "Christ Has No Body But Yours–St. Teresa of Avila." *CatholicLink*. December/18/2024. https://catholic-link.org/quotes/st-teresa-of-avila-quote-christ-has-no-body-but-yours.

4 St. Francis of Assisi. "Prayer of St. Francis of Assisi (Prayer for Peace)." *The Cathedral of Saint Thomas More*. December/18/2024. https://www.cathedralstm.org/about-our-catholic-faith/expressing-our-faith/treasury-catholic-prayers/prayer-st-francis-assisi-prayer-peace.

5 Merton, Thomas. "Prologue" in *No Man Is an Island*. New York: Harcourt, Inc., 1983.

6 My sister Gloria Renollet facilitates intergroup dialogue (IGD) workshops founded on Weisel's quote. You can learn more about her work, including a TEDx Talk inspired by her time in the Middle East, here: https://www.gloriarenollet.com.

7 Seligson, Susan. "Elie Weisel (Hon. '74), Spokesman for Peace and Human Rights, Dies at 87." *Bostonia*. July/3/2016. December/18/2024.

8 Kierkegaard, Søren. "What Meaning and What Joy There Are in the Thought of Following Christ" in *Upbuilding Discourses in Various Spirits*. Edited and translated by Howard V. Hong and Edna H. Hong. Princeton: Princeton University Press, 1993. *Kierkegaard's Writings, XV, Volume 15: Upbuilding Discourses in Various Spirits*. Princeton: Princeton University Press, 2009. https://muse.jhu.edu/book/46419.

9 II Corinthians 2:15-17

10 O'Donohue, John. "The Mystery of Friendship" in *Anam Cara: A Book of Celtic Wisdom*. New York: Cliff Street Books, 1997.

11 Theopedia. "Saint." *Theopedia*. December/18/2024. https://www.theopedia.com/saint#:~:text=In%20the%20Bible%2C%20the%20word%20saint%20comes%20from,apart%20or%20made%20holy%20by%20faith%20in%20Christ.

12 Genesis 6:9 (NLT)

13 Genesis 12:1 (ESV) Unless otherwise noted, I used ESV for all biblical references.

14 Ruth 1

15 Genesis 37, 39-50

16 Exodus 2-3, Exodus 14-17, Numbers 11-12, 14, 16, 20-21, Deuteronomy 34

17 Esther 2

18 Jeremiah 38

19 Matthew 3:7

20 St. John of the Cross. "Prologue" in *Dark Night of the Soul: A Masterpiece in the Literature of Mysticism by St. John of the Cross*. Edited by E. Allison Peers. New York: Image Books Doubleday, 1990.

21 Donlon, Charlotte. "Linger and Listen" in *The Great Belonging: How Loneliness Leads Us to Each Other*. Minneapolis: Broadleaf Books, 2020.

22 Donlon, Charlotte. "Receiving Grace" in *The Great Belonging: How Loneliness Leads Us to Each Other*. Minneapolis: Broadleaf Books, 2020.

23 Herbert, George. "Love (3)" in *The Complete English Works*. New York: Alfred A. Knopf, 1995.

culled salt: on saying goodbye

1 Genesis 1:31

2 St. Anselm. *Complete Philosophical and Theological Treatises of Anselm of Canterbury*. Translated by Jasper Hopkins and Herbert Richardson. Minneapolis: The Arthur J. Banning Press, 2000. E-book. https://antilogicalism.com/wp-content/uploads/2018/04/proslogion.pdf.

3 King, Martin Luther. "Letter from a Birmingham Jail" in *Letters to a Birmingham Jail: A Response to the Words and Dreams of Dr. Martin Luther King, Jr.* Chicago: Moody Publishers, 2014.

4 Psalm 51:1

5 Matthew 27:46

6 Chesterton, G.K. "Introduction" in *The Everlasting Man*. Seaside, Oregon: Rough Draft Printing, 2013.

7 Vodolazkin, Eugene. *Laurus*. London: Oneworld Publications, 2016.

the blissful abyss: on boredom

1 I Corinthians 13:1-3

2 Ecclesiastes 1:9

3 "Money, ambition, consideration, celebrity, power, our loved ones, everything that puts into us the capacity for action is like bread. If any one of these attachments penetrates deeply enough into us to reach the vital roots of our carnal existence, its loss may break us and even cause our death. That is called dying of love. It is like dying of hunger." Weil, Simone. "Concerning the Our Father" in *Waiting for God*. New York: Harper and Row, Publishers, 1973. PDF.

4 James 1:15

5 Psalm 123:2

vanished flights and snow days: on cancellations

1 Woldeyes, Eleni. "Insider's Guide to Vegan Ethiopian Food." *The Nomadic Vegan*. August/9/2020. *December/19/2024.* https://www.thenomadicvegan.com/vegan-ethiopian-food.

2 Macrotrends. "Ethiopia Poverty Rate 1995-2024." *Macrotrends.* December/19/2024. https://www.macrotrends.net/global-metrics/countries/ETH/ethiopia/poverty-rate.

3 I Thessalonians 5:17

4 May, Katherine. "Snow" in *Wintering: The Power of Rest and Retreat in Difficult Times*. New York: Riverhead Books, 2020.

5 See: Wirzba, Norman. "The 'Roots' of Eating: Our Life Together in Gardens" in *Food and Faith: A Theology of Eating*. Cambridge: Cambridge University Press, 2011.

6 Leviticus 25:1-7

7 Leviticus 25:8-17

8 Blackman, Jessie and Roberts, Susha. "Seven Feasts That Point to Christ." *Wycliffe Bible Translators*. December/19/2024.

9 Strong, James. "H7673" in *Strong's Exhaustive Concordance of the Bible*, Updated and Expanded Edition. Peabody, Massachusetts: Hendrickson Publishers, 2007.

10 Exodus 20:8-11

11 Exodus 35:2

12 Jeremiah 17:27

13 Ezekiel 20:21-24

14 Ezekiel 20:13

15 Genesis 6:9

16 Luke 5:16

17 Colossians 2:9

18 Philippians 2:5-11

19 Pietrangelo, Ann. "The Effects of Stress on Your Body." *Healthline*. March/21/2023. 19/December/2024. https://www.healthline.com/health/stress/effects-on-body.

20 World Population Review. "Depression Rates by Country 2024." *World Population Review*. 19/December/2024. https://worldpopulationreview.com/country-rankings/depression-rates-by-country.

21 Pederson, Cate. "The Fallow Fields." *Modern Agriculture*. December/6/2015. December/19/2024. https://modernagriculture.ca/research/fallow-fields.

22 Pease, Roland. "Dust Bowl 2.0? Rising Great Plains dust levels stir concerns." *Science*. October/20/2020. December/18/2024. https://www.science.org/content/article/dust-bowl-20-rising-great-plains-dust-levels-stir-concerns.

23 History.com Editors. "Dust Bowl." *History.* April/24/2023. December/19/2024. https://www.history.com/topics/great-depression/dust-bowl.

24 Greenspan, Jesse. "What Happened on Black Sunday?" *History.* April/13/2020. December/19/2020. https://www.history.com/news/remembering-black-sunday.

25 Leviticus 25:4

26 In a Sabbath year, the land is open for communal partaking (Leviticus 25).

27 Psalm 131

28 James 4:13-15

29 Julian of Norwich. "The Thirteenth Revelation" in *Revelations of Divine Love.* New York: Penguin Books, 1966.

kitchen tabernacles: on hunger

1 World Health Organization. "UN Report: Global hunger numbers rose to as many as 828 million in 2021." *World Health Organization.* July/6/2022. December/19/2024.

2 I Corinthians 10:31

3 Gibran, Kahlil. "On Eating and Drinking" in *The Prophet.* London: Arcturus Publishing Limited, 2023.

4 Psalm 34:8

5 Wirzba, Norman. "The 'Roots' of Eating: Our Life Together in Gardens" in *Food and Faith: A Theology of Eating.* Cambridge: Cambridge University Press, 2011.

6 Weil, Simone. "Forms of the Implicit Love of God" in *Waiting for God.* New York: Harper and Row, Publishers, 1973. PDF. "The love of this beauty proceeds from God dwelling in our souls and goes out to God present in the universe. It also is like a sacrament."

7 Capon, Robert Farrar. "The Generous Ox" in *The Supper of the Lamb: A Culinary Reflection*. New York: The Modern Library, 2002.

8 Ibid.

9 Berry, Wendell. "The Gift of Good Land" in *The Gift of Good Land: Further Essays Cultural and Agricultural*. New York: North Point Press, 1981.

10 United Nations. "'Outrageous a Person Dies of Hunger Every Few Seconds', Secretary-General Declares in Message on World Food Day, Calls for Crisis to Be Top of Global Agenda." *United Nations*. October/6/2023. December/20/2024. https://press.un.org/en/2023/sgsm21980.doc.htm.

11 Exodus 16

12 Weil, Simone."Concerning the Our Father" in *Waiting for God*. New York: Harper and Row, Publishers, 1973. PDF. "We cannot bind our will today for tomorrow; we cannot make a pact with him that tomorrow he will be within us, even in spite of ourselves. Our consent to his presence is the same as his presence. Consent is an act; it can only be actual, that is to say, in the present."

13 Brother Lawrence. *The Practice of the Presence of God*. New Kensington, Pennsylvania: Whitaker House, 1982.

14 Laubach, Frank. *Letters by a Modern Mystic*. Colorado Springs: Purposeful Design Publications, 2007.

15 I Thessalonians 5:17

16 Weil, Simone. "Concerning the Our Father" in *Waiting for God*. New York: Harper and Row, Publishers, 1973. PDF.

17 II Samuel 11

18 Weil, Simone. "Concerning the Our Father" in *Waiting for God*. New York: Harper and Row, Publishers, 1973. PDF. "Money, ambition, consideration, celebrity, power, our loved ones, everything that puts into us the capacity for action is like bread. If any one of these attachments penetrates deeply enough into us to reach the vital roots of our carnal existence, its loss may break us and even cause our death. That is called dying of love. It is like dying of hunger."

19 Wirzba, Norman. "Life through Death: Sacrificial Eating" in *Food and Faith: A Theology of Eating*. Cambridge: Cambridge University Press, 2011.

20 Weil, Simone. "Forms of the Implicit Love of God" in *Waiting for God*. New York: Harper and Row, Publishers, 1973. PDF.

21 Pascal, Blaise. *Pensées*. Paris: Librairie Générale Française, 1972.

22 Psalm 30:5

23 Matthew 4:4

24 Wirzba, Norman. "Life Through Death" in *Food and Faith: A Theology of Eating*. Cambridge: Cambridge University Press, 2011.

25 John 15:5

26 Merton, Thomas. "The Inward Solitude" in *No Man Is an Island*. New York: Harcourt, Inc., 1983.

27 Numbers 21

28 Wirzba, Norman. "Life through Death: Sacrificial Eating" in *Food and Faith: A Theology of Eating*. Cambridge: Cambridge University Press, 2011.

29 Merton, Thomas. "Asceticism and Sacrifice" in *No Man Is an Island*. New York: Harcourt, Inc., 1983.

30 Psalm 34:10

31 Matthew 5:6

32 John 6:35, John 4:10–13
33 Luke 1:53

34 Weil, Simone. "Forms of the Implicit Love of God" in *Waiting for God*. New York: Harper and Row, Publishers, 1973. PDF. "The great trouble in human life is that looking and eating are two different operations. Only beyond the sky, in the country inhabited by God, are they one and the same operation."

35 II Corinthians 4:7

36 I Corinthians 13:12

the garden queue: on waiting

1 Merton, Thomas. "The Inward Solitude" in *No Man Is an Island*. New York: Harcourt, Inc., 1983.

2 Exodus 20:2

3 St. John of the Cross. "The Dark Night of the Soul." *The Contemplative Life.* November/19/2017. January/8/2025. https://www.thecontemplativelife.org/blog/ascent-of-mount-carmel-fired-with-loves-urgent-longings.

veiled faces: on unknowing

1 Proverbs 9:10

2 Isaiah 42:18

3 *Online Etymology Dictionary*. "Mystery (n.1)." *Online Etymology Dictionary.* December/20/2024. https://www.etymonline.com/word/mystery.

4 Lewis, C.S. "Eight" in *Till We Have Faces: A Myth Retold*. New York: Harcourt, Brace and Company, 1956.
5 Ibid, 123.

6 Ibid, 136.

7 Isaiah 31:1

8 Ibid, 244.

9 Isaiah 42:16

10 Isaiah 50:10–11

11 Lewis, C.S. "Fifteen" in *Till We Have Faces: A Myth Retold*. New York: Harcourt, Brace and Company, 1956.

12 Song of Solomon 1:7

13 Isaiah 30:28a

14 Isaiah 27:1

15 Isaiah 28:21

16 Isaiah 29:11-12

17 Isaiah 30:30

18 "The Valley of Vision" in *The Valley of Vision: A Collection of Puritan Prayers & Devotions*." Edited by Arthur Bennett. Carlisle, Pennsylvania: The Banner of Truth Trust, 1975.

19 "The Third Chapter" in *The Cloud of Unknowing*, Golden Library Edition. Springfield: Templegate, 1964.

20 St. John of the Cross." Chapter XII: Of the benefits which the night causes in the soul" in *Dark Night of the Soul: A Masterpiece in the Literature of Mysticism by St. John of the Cross*. Edited by E. Allison Peers. New York: Image Books Doubleday, 1990.
21 St. John of the Cross. "Prologue" in *Dark Night of the Soul: A Masterpiece in the Literature of Mysticism by St. John of the Cross*. Edited by E. Allison Peers. New York: Image Books Doubleday, 1990.

22 Merton, Thomas. "Christmas, 1941 (Before Midnight Mass) in *Meditations, December 23-30, 1941*. PDF.

23 Lewis, C.S. "Twenty-One" in *Till We Have Faces: A Myth Retold*. New York: Harcourt, Brace and Company, 1956."But to hint and hover, to draw near us in dreams and oracles, or in a waking vision that vanishes as soon as seen, to be dead silent when we question them and then glide back and whisper (words we cannot understand) in our ears when we most wish to be free of them, and to show to one what they hid from another; what is all this but cat-and-mouse play, blind man's buff, and mere jugglery? Why must holy places be dark places?"

24 Isaiah 34

25 Isaiah 32:3

26 Psalm 131

27 See: Smith, Cyprian. *The Way of Paradox: Spiritual Life as Taught by Meister Eckhart*, New Edition. London: Darton, Longman and Todd Ltd., 2014.

28 Weil, Simone. "Hesitations Concerning Baptism" in *Waiting for God*. New York: Harper and Row, Publishers, 1973. PDF.

29 Lewis, C.S. "Ten" in *Till We Have Faces: A Myth Retold*. New York: Harcourt, Brace and Company, 1956.

30 Revelation 14:2, Ezekiel 43:2

31 Lewis, C.S. "Four" in *Till We Have Faces: A Myth Retold*. New York: Harcourt, Brace and Company, 1956.

holy houseflies: on annoyances

1 Ecclesiastes 1:2

2 Lamentations 3:22-23

3 James 4:1-3

4 Christian Classics Ethereal Library. "Letter XXIII. Sensitiveness under reproof the surest sign we needed it" in *Spiritual Progress*. Fénelon, François. 1/January/2025. https://ccel.org/ccel/fenelon/progress/progress.iv.xxiv.html.

5 Lewis, C.S. "Let's Pretend" in *Mere Christianity*. New York: Harper One, 2001.

6 Mark 5:25–34

7 Bonhoeffer, Dietrich. "The Ministry of Helpfulness" in *Life Together: The Classic Exploration of Christian Community*. New York: HarperOne, 2009.

8 See: L'Engle, Madeleine. "Keeping the Clock Wound" in *Walking on Water: Reflections on Faith and Art*. New York: Convergent Books, 2016.

jet skis in a storm: on fear

1 Centers for Disease Control and Prevention. "Pregnant and Recently Pregnant People at Increased Risk for Severe Illness from COVID-19." *Centers for Disease Control and Prevention.* October/25/2022. December/21/2024. https://archive.cdc.gov/#/details?q=pregnant%20and%20recently%20pregnant%20people%20covid&start=0&rows=10&url=https://www.cdc.gov/coronavirus/2019-ncov/need-extra-precautions/pregnant-people.html.

2 Centers for Disease Control and Prevention. "Emerging Threats to Mothers and Babies." *Centers for Disease Control and Prevention.* May/15/2024. December/21/2024. https://www.cdc.gov/set-net/php/articles-and-key-findings/?CDC_AAref_Val=https://www.cdc.gov/ncbddd/set-net/articles.html.

3 Psalm 46

4 Weil, Simone. "The Love of God and Affliction" in *The Simone Weil Reader.* Edited by George A. Panichas. New York: David McKay Company, Inc., 1977.

5 Exodus 3-4:14

6 Jeremiah 1:4-10

7 Jeremiah 51:54

a long and chilly vigil: on winter

1 Norris, Kathleen. "Dreaming of Trees" in *The Cloister Walk.* New York: Riverhead Books, 1996.

2 L'Engle, Madeleine. *A Circle of Quiet.* New York: Open Road Media, 2017.

3 May, Katherine. "Snow" in *Wintering: The Power of Rest and Retreat in Difficult Times.* New York: Riverhead Books, 2020.

4 Ibid, 13.

5 National Coalition for the Homeless. "National Coalition for the Homeless Calls for Warming Centers to be Opened in US Cities to Meet Demand!" *National Coalition for the Homeless.* December/21/2024. https://nationalhomeless.org/tag/hypothermia.

6 MacLaughlin, Nina. "Inhale the Darkness" in *Winter Solstice.* Boston: Black Sparrow Press, 2023.

7 Ibid, 69.

8 Norris, Kathleen. "Dreaming of Trees" in *The Cloister Walk.* New York: Riverhead Books, 1996.

laundry and liturgy: on cleaning

1 Exodus 19:10

2 Numbers 19:18

3 Exodus 31:17-21

4 Revelation 7:14

5 Psalm 84:1

6 Norris, Kathleen. The Quotidian Mysteries: *Laundry, Liturgy and "Women's Work."* New York: Paulist Press, 1998.

7 Ezekiel 16:1-14

8 Bible Hub. "2889. Kosmos." *Bible Hub.* 21/December/2024. https://biblehub.com/greek/2889.html.

9 John 20:6-7

10 Norris, Kathleen. *The Quotidian Mysteries: Laundry, Liturgy and "Women's Work."* New York: Paulist Press, 1998.

11 John 13:1-17

12 Chittister, Joan. "The Daily Manual Labor" in *The Rule of Benedict: A Spirituality for the 21st Century*. New York: The Crossroad Publishing Company, 2010.

13 II Corinthians 5:21

14 Christianity Today." Brother Lawrence: Practitioner of God's presence." *Christianity Today*. August/8/2008. January/3/2025. https://www.christianitytoday.com/2008/08/brother-lawrence.

15 Mathias, Anita. "Brother Lawrence, Living in Heaven on Earth." *Anita Mathias*. May/28/2010. Jamuary/9/2015. https://anitamathias.com/2010/05/28/brother-lawrence-living-in-heaven-on-earth.
Brother Lawrence is thought to have penned this lovely prayer for (as my grandmother would say) chief cooks and bottle washers:

O Lord of pots and pans and things,
Since I have no time to be
a great saint by doing lovely things,
or watching late with Thee,
or dreaming in the dawnlight,
or storming Heaven's gates,
Make me a saint by getting meals,
and washing up the plates.
Warm all the kitchen with Thy Love,
and light it with Thy peace;
Forgive me all my worrying,
and make my grumbling cease.
Thou who didst love to give men food
in room, or by the sea,
Accept the service that I do—
I do it unto Thee.

the wakeful desert: on sleep deprivation

1 Ryrie, Alexander. "Introduction: The Desert Movement" in *The Desert Movement: Fresh Perspectives on the Spirituality of the Desert*.

2 Ward, Benedicta, translator. "Foreword" in *Sayings of the Desert Fathers*. Kalamazoo: Cistercian Publications, 1984. PDF.

3 Ryrie, Alexander. "The Way of the Desert" in T*he Desert Movement: Fresh Perspectives on the Spirituality of the Desert.*

4 Ryrie, Alexander."Upper Egypt" in *The Desert Movement: Fresh Perspectives on the Spirituality of the Desert.* Norwich: Canterbury Press, 2011.

5 Ward, Benedicta, translator. "Arsenius" in *Sayings of the Desert Fathers.* Kalamazoo: Cistercian Publications, 1984. PDF.

6 Ibid.

7 Ward, Benedicta, translator. "Bessarion" in *Sayings of the Desert Fathers.* Kalamazoo: Cistercian Publications, 1984. PDF.

8 I Kings 3:12

9 Psalm 127:2

10 Psalm 3:5

11 Matthew 14:23; Mark 1:35; Luke 5:16

12 Mark 4:38-40

13 Genesis 1:4-5

14 Ward, Benedicta, translator. "Poemen (called the Shepherd)" in *Sayings of the Desert Fathers.* Kalamazoo: Cistercian Publications, 1984. PDF.

15 Zechariah 4

16 Ephesians 6:12

17 Ward, Benedicta, translator. "Amtnonas" in *Sayings of the Desert Fathers.* Kalamazoo: Cistercian Publications, 1984. PDF.

18 Ibid.

19 Malvern Museum of Local History. "Daily Routines of Benedictine Monks." *Malvern Museum of Local History.* April/2/2019. Daily routines of Benedictine Monks (malvernmuseum.co.uk).

20 Ward, Benedicta, translator. "Syncletica" in *Sayings of the Desert Fathers*. Kalamazoo: Cistercian Publications, 1984.

21 Psalm 63:6

22 Psalm 119:62

23 Luke 12:32

24 Acts 16:25

25 Cline, John. "The Desert, Sleep, and the Mystical Experience." *Psychology Today*. September/14/2014. December/23/2024. https://www.psychologytoday.com/us/blog/sleepless-in-america/201409/the-desert-sleep-and-the-mystical-experience.

26 May, Katherine. "Slumber" in *Wintering: The Power of Rest and Retreat in Difficult Times*. New York: Riverhead Books, 2020. Here May describes how writing in the middle of the night gives rise to insights.

27 "The Third Chapter" in *The Cloud of Unknowing*, Golden Library Edition. Springfield: Templegate, 1964.

28 "The Fifth Chapter" in *The Cloud of Unknowing*, Golden Library Edition. Springfield: Templegate, 1964.

29 Funk, Mary Margaret. "About Acedia" in *Thoughts Matter: The Practice of the Spiritual Life*. New York: Continuum, 1998.
30 Nouwen, Henri. "A Heart that Embraces the Universe" in *The Only Necessary Thing: Living a Prayerful Life*. New York: The Crossroad Publishing Company, 1999.

31 Kierkegaard, Søren. Translated by Alastair Hannay. "Preamble from the Heart" in *Fear and Trembling*. New York: Penguin Books, 2006.

pinned thorax: on pain

1 Alvarez, Julia. *In the Time of the Butterflies*. Chapel Hill: Algonquin Books, 2010.

2 Gibran, Kahlil. "On Pain" in *The Prophet*. London: Arcturus Publishing Limited, 2023.

3 Or, as Simone Weil has it, "It is God himself holding his hand and pressing it rather hard." Weil, Simone. "Affliction and the Love of God" in *The Simone Weil Reader*. Edited by George A. Panichas. New York: David McKay Company, Inc., 1977.

4 Isaiah 53:3-5

5 "We can be thankful not only for [our] fragility itself but also for that more intimate weakness which connects it with the very centre of our being. For it is this weakness which makes possible, in certain conditions, the operation by which we are nailed to the very centre of the Cross." Weil, Simone. "The Love of God and Affliction" in *The Simone Weil Reader*. Edited by George A. Panichas. New York: David McKay Company, Inc., 1977.

6 Moore, Caroline. "The Wonder of Moths." *Plough*. July/22/2024. December/23/2024. https://www.plough.com/en/topics/justice/environment/the-wonder-of-moths. Moths are highly fragile and some of the planet's most sensitive creatures to environmental disaster.

7 Blake, William. "On Another's Sorrow" in *The Complete Poetry and Prose of William Blake*. New York: Anchor Books, 1982.

8 Lewis, C. S. "How the Adventure Ended" in *The Voyage of the Dawn Treader*. New York: HarperCollins Publishers, 1980.

9 Hart, David Bentley. *The Doors of the Sea: Where Was God in the Tsunami*. Grand Rapids: Wm. B. Eerdmans Publishing Co., 2011.

about the author

 Elise Tegegne is a writer and editor. She holds an MFA in Creative Writing from Seattle Pacific University, and her work has appeared in *Plough*, *Ekstasis* by *Christianity Today*, *Dappled Things*, *The Windhover*, *Risen Motherhood*, and *The Indianapolis Star*, among others. She taught French in Addis Ababa, Ethiopia, where she met her husband. She now lives in Indianapolis with her family. Find her on social media @ elisetegegne or on her website, www.elisetegegne.com.